COLLECTED POEMS: 3

Peter Reading: Collected Poems

1: POEMS 1970-1984 (Bloodaxe Books, 1995)

INTRODUCTION by Isabel Martin
Water and Waste (1970)
For the Municipality's Elderly (1974)
The Prison Cell & Barrel Mystery (1976)
Nothing For Anyone (1977)
Fiction (1979)
Tom o' Bedlam's Beauties (1981)
Diplopic (1983)
5x5x5x5x5 (1983)
C (1984)

2: POEMS 1985-1996 (Bloodaxe Books, 1996)

Ukulele Music (1985)
Going On (1985)
Stet (1986)
Final Demands (1988)
Perduta Gente (1989)
Shitheads (1989)
Evagatory (1992)
Last Poems (1994)
Eschatological (1996)
INDEX OF TITLES AND FIRST LINES TO VOLS 1 & 2

3: POEMS 1997-2003 (Bloodaxe Books, 2003)

Work in Regress (1997)
Ob. (1999)
Marfan (2000)
[untitled] (2001)
Faunal (2002)
Civil (2002)
♩ (2003)
INDEX OF TITLES AND FIRST LINES TO VOL 3

RECORDINGS

The Poetry Quartets: 3 (Bloodaxe Books/British Council, 1998)
  [with James Fenton, Tony Harrison & Ken Smith: 30 mins each]
The Life Works of Peter Reading (Lannan Foundation, 2003)
  [22 DVD videos: total length 22 hours: *see* www.lannan.org]

—PETER READING—
Collected Poems

3: POEMS 1997-2003

BLOODAXE BOOKS

ISBN: 1 85224 624 3 hardback edition
       1 85224 625 1 paperback edition

First published 2003 by
Bloodaxe Books Ltd,
Highgreen,
Tarset,
Northumberland NE48 1RP.

www.bloodaxebooks.com
For further information about Bloodaxe titles
please visit our website or write to
the above address for a catalogue.

Bloodaxe Books Ltd acknowledges
the financial assistance of
Arts Council England, North East.

Cover printing by J. Thomson Colour Printers Ltd, Glasgow.

Printed in Great Britain by
Cromwell Press Ltd, Trowbridge, Wiltshire.

To William Johnston

(The old ones descry,
by evening's impartial glim,
that which the mirrors imply.)

ACKNOWLEDGEMENTS

The first five books of volume 3 of Peter Reading's *Collected Poems* were first published as individual collections by Bloodaxe Books as follows: *Work in Regress* (1997), *Ob.* (1999), *Marfan* (2000), *[untitled]* (2001) and *Faunal* (2002).

Civil was commissioned by BBC Radio 3 for broadcast in 2002. The new collection *ʒ* (2003) is previously unpublished, and includes some poems which first appeared in *Metre*, *Poetry Review* and the *Times Literary Supplement*.

The photographs in *Marfan* are by Jay Shuttleworth. All other artwork is by Peter Reading. The poem 'Alert!' in *[untitled]* is Reading's version from an English rendering by Armenian writer Vahé Oshagan (1922-2000) of his own poem.

An introduction to the author's work by Isabel Martin appears at the front of volume 1 of *Collected Poems*. An combined index to the first two volumes can be found at the back of volume 2.

Recordings of Peter Reading reading all three volumes of his *Collected Poems* are also available as *The Life Works of Peter Reading* (Lannan Foundation, 2003). For full details of the 22 DVD video set, *see* www.lannan.org. The audio files of these recordings (the entire 22 hours filmed over a week at Highgreen Manor) can be accessed from the Lannan website.

Lannan: *fons et origo.*

CONTENTS

OB. (1999)

MARFAN (2000)

CIVIL (2002)

𝄞 (2003)

All poems are untitled:

WORK IN REGRESS

(1997)

*(Desperate Circumstances
demand disparate measures.)*

Three

1946:
the first post-war bananas
arrive in Britain; Churchill
receives the Order of Merit;
three-year-old treated to four
bananas dies of the overdose;
Government plans to spend
380 million
on building 'New Towns' to 'encourage
a sense of culture and pride
in those who will live in them';
the Jitterbug hits Brit ballrooms;
John Logie Baird dies;
H.G. Wells dies;
Granville Bantock dies;
Hermann Goering dies;
W.C. Fields dies;
Ladislao Biro invents
the ball-point pen; the Beeb
engenders the Third Programme;
Peter Reading is born.

*

'70: 4,000 Brits
die of Asian flu
in week ending January 2nd;
Bertrand Russell dies
aged 97; Nixon
sends US troops to Cambodia;
E.M. Forster dies;
the great Mark Rothko dies;
Heath is elected PM;
Tynan concocts *Oh! Calcutta!*
Palestinian hijackers
blow up some Boeings (of course);
Mary Wilson (Harold's
missus) publishes poems
(price 12 shillings, nice);

missiles are hurled at the stage
during the Miss World contest;
Pravda slams Solzhenitsyn...

Also, George MacBeth
is presenting *Poetry Now*
on the wireless's Third Programme
and invites Peter Reading
to Broadcasting House to record
his own valedictory poem
in his own ugly voice
(half-a-lifetime younger):
Evenings are drawing in quickly,
we sip dry Sherry, it darkens,
decanters of Sauternes for plasma,
the central heating is love-fired
against the chill of the evenings,
evenings are drawing in quickly...
In the BBC Club an hour later,
sipping a Fino or two,
George recalls early days
and working with Louis MacNeice,
remarks how, though he once shared
an office with him, he never
felt that he knew the loner.
Then, naturally, the chat
turns to grim Demise.
MacBeth posits his theory
that friends who happen to die
are merely the same as those
whom we know to exist but don't see.
Well, *maybe*, Reading opines,
and commits the hypothesis
to oblivion, till, years later,
his best mate is flensed in a car crash
and his own ugly voice
records in a monotone:
You used Propertius once
to Preface a ghost poem – Sunt
aliquid manes, letum
non omnia finit...

And now George MacBeth himself
(who, somehow, seemed unassailable
by mortal distemper) is dead,
and Reading remembers the Langham,
the talk and the subsequent tapes,
and hears his own ugly voice
(half-a-life younger) and George
mispronouncing 'Reading',
and regrets that he failed on that
and other occasions to say
'Thank you, George, and goodbye'.

*

1971:
Sonny Liston dies;
Idi Amin stages coup;
the great Stravinsky dies;
Arsenal wins the Cup;
Ogden Nash dies;
Louis Armstrong dies;
riots flare in Ulster;
first Baron Reith dies;
Northern Ireland – another
1,500 troops
are sent to the bloody province;
BBC swamped with complaints
when a boy uses four-letter-word
on, of all things, *Woman's Hour*;
Nikita Khrushchev dies;
the hits of '71 –
'My Sweet Lord', 'Maggie May',
and 'Chirpy, Chirpy, Cheep, Cheep'…

And I listen again to the voices –
George MacBeth mispronouncing
'Reading' and Reading reading
half-a-life younger, stridulous:
*All must return to our dusty
origins sometime, all
must return to our dusty origins…*

*

1980: Sir Cecil
Beaton pops his clogs;
Graham Sutherland dies;
Oskar Kokoschka dies;
Hitchcock and Tito die;
Iranian Embassy stormed;
Henbit wins the Derby;
Henry Miller dies;
Peter Sellers dies;
Iraq attacks Iran;
Iran attacks Iraq;
Jeremy Isaacs chosen
to head fourth TV channel;
fuck knows who shot JR;
Oswald Mosley, friend
of Mussolini and Hitler,
dies (somewhat belatedly)...

and the voice of George MacBeth
from sixteen years ago
announces 'Alma Mater',
to be followed by nasal growlings...

Sunt aliquid manes.

*

1982:
civil unrest in Bristol;
Thelonious Monk dies;
Carl Orff and 'Rab' Butler die;
Argentina invades the Falklands;
Israel invades Lebanon;
Henry Fonda dies;
Ingrid Bergman dies;
Group Captain Bader dies;
Glenn Gould dies;
Jacques Tati dies;
Arthur Askey dies;
'Bad Language' on Channel 4!;
man gets mechanical heart;
the women at Greenham Common
are carted away by Old Bill;

Reading is reading 'Dark Continent'
and 'The Terrestrial Globe'...

*

1984:
Johnny Weissmuller dies;
the halfpenny piece is phased out;
acid rain threatens UK;
Torvill and Dean win a gold
at the Sarajevo Olympics;
William 'Count' Basie dies;
Tito Gobbi dies;
Sir John Betjeman dies;
Eric Morecambe dies;
at last!, the 'Greenhouse Effect';
the level of childhood leukaemia
is ten times the national average
around Sellafield nuclear plant;
James F. Fixx (the man
who turned America on
to jogging) dies (while jogging)
of a massive heart attack;
J.B. Priestley dies;
Truman Capote dies;
Richard Burton dies;
Islamic suicide bomber
kills 40 in US Embassy
in mad bloody East Beirut;
Indira Gandhi shot dead;
famine in Ethiopia;
Reagan romps to victory.

The hits of '84:
'I just called to say I love you',
'Do they know it's Christmas?', 'Relax'.

On BBC Radio 3,
Reading is reading a poem
concerning the hapless fishermen
caught in the blast and fall
of the Bikini explosion
(Sunt aliquid manes)...

*

1996:
Reading recording this,
thinks of George MacBeth's proposition
that friends who happen to die
are merely the same as those
whom we know to exist but don't see,
Sunt aliquid manes,
letum non omnia finit,
and is assailed by the voices,
Sunt aliquid manes,
letum non omnia finit,
and the rewinds, stops, fast-forwards,
and thinks of how Gavin Ewart
(avuncular, unassuming,
genial eroticist,
laureate of levity,
champ of the flyweight poem,
angry, compassionate, sensitive,
at once amused and appalled)
would have been 80 this year...

and thinks how the carnage continues,
and of how he will soon be part of it,
Sunt aliquid manes,

Sunt aliquid manes,

Sunt aliquid manes,

Sunt aliquid manes,

Sunt aliquid manes,

Sunt aliquid manes,

Sunt aliquid manes,

Sunt aliquid manes,

Sunt aliquid manes...

Fireworks

The shelling is heavy tonight;
if we survive till tomorrow
there'll be nettle soup and black bread.

Shropshire Lads

Thick mist enswathes the Prison at Shrewsbury;
a bloke I know inside would dearly wish
to be on this train bound for benign Ludlow.

*

Places of interest in this town include:
Ludlow Museum, Ludlow Castle... [and
the Hen & Chickens, where, each Friday night,
the Smiths and Bradleys thump each other shitless].

The farewell,

the fumbled embrace,
the suddenly otiose kiss,
the Tannoy *regrets that this...*
twenty-eight years late,
the solo stroll to the end
of the platform wherefrom the sleepers
recede and recede and recede.

Mimnermian [Mimnermus (*fl.* 630 BC)]

Just as new petals sparkling in springtime
    quicken in sunlight,
        so do we burgeon in youth
        reckless of impartial Zeus.

Two Fates attend us: one is the bane, the
    fruit of our dotage;
        one is the blessing of death
        ending our nonage's bloom.

When the brief blossom is done, to die is
    better than living
        haplessly plagued by the dread
        of penury, grief and the grave.

Painful longevity, chance death early,
    death of one's children –
        infinite is the ill-luck
        on the Olympian list.

Seed

Onto the pile of the Axminster fluffs of
   willowherb settle.
      Autumn: the wanton swing-doors
      splay to admit this spent seed.

Shakespearean

Someone I know was lolling in the doorway
of a stuffy factory office where he worked
absorbing early April UV rays
when down the yard the General Manager
came striding clad in a protective white
crisp overall against industrial grime.
The gaffer twitched an eyebrow then observed:
'I see you *like* the sun; a nice bright day?'
The idler laconically riposted:
'It is the bright day that brings forth the adder;
and that craves wary walking.' One week later
Head Office sent him his P45.

Nomenclature

The marriage vows:
Lead Albatross.

The only child:
A Second Chance.

The railway fare:
Pence on the Tongue.

The air-hostess:
Grim Charonis.

The civic bronze:
Persephone.

Ovidian

Banished, maybe, but the fame of Naso
   possibly lives on
      still in the City where men
      mention my name with respect.

Those who still spare me a thought should know the
   fate I endure here
      on this forgotten stark shore
      under the frost-sharpened stars.

I am surrounded by hordes of barbarians –
   which tribe is foulest
      I am unable to judge
      for they seem equally vile.

In the short summer the river protects us
      from an invasion
            but, when it freezes, the hordes
            cross the thick ice to maraud.

Snow falling constantly whipped by the wind lies
      heavy and hardens,
            sun will not thaw it, nor rain,
            more falls and settles on top.

Here the indigenous swaddle themselves in
      pelts of the wild beasts –
            all one can see is their beards
            riddled with sparkling rime.

Wine freezes hard, the bottle-shaped lumps they
      cleave with machetes,
            serving it solid to suck,
            crunch on or melt in the mouth.

Water is chiselled like stone from the lakes; the
      Danube is hard-paved;
            where the boats bobbed, horses pound,
            trundling oxen-carts cross;

even the sea ices over – I've often
      walked on its surface
            slithering on the tough shell
            safe from the water beneath

(now, had the Hellespont been so composed, the
      hapless Leander
            could have walked calmly across
            wisely eschewing the waves);

dolphins, unable to arch from the brine, are
      trapped by the ice crust;
            breakers, solidified, grasp
            shipping and fish in a vice.

Over the ice-bridge as soon as it forms the
    barbarous horsemen
        gallop with thunderous strength,
        whipping their steeds into froth,

pillaging, savagely sacking the farmsteads,
    taking the women.
        Villagers, terrified, hide,
        flee from the venom-barbed shafts.

Then the marauders swoop on the prize of
    untended livestock,
        implements, carts and such things,
        leaving the hovels in flames.

Those who are taken and tied up turn to
    see their homes blazing;
        that which the raiders don't want
        they systematically wreck.

After the raid the survivors remain in
    great trepidation,
        loth to return to the plough,
        dreading another attack,

so that the fields lie abandoned and always
    barren and blighted –
        no vineyards, no foamy vats,
        no orchards bearing rich fruit.

This is a land where, unless a man is
    dogged by misfortune,
        he should not venture to be;
        my lot it is to live here.

Horatian

Nunc est bibendum
(then address the issue of
  cheesy pudendum).

Integration

Between the Bookie and the Balti House
a grim homunculus purveys the *Echo*,
but periodically he sallies forth
to cow his patrons with a raised clenched fist,
and they are clearly discomposed by this.

The, ahem, Hospital *discharged him early –*
they have a serious shortage of resources...

He's been ensconced here for about two years
and we take something from him every day,
and by this regular sociability
it's hoped we all shall soon be integrated.

Nips

'No,' I replied when
my Aunt Prudence said to me
'Give up the drink,' '*No.*'

*

Chaos rife outside;
I fuss about in the house
tidying things up.

*

Ill-concealed contempt
is, perhaps, what I evinced
when the rep. walked in.

*

Everybody knows
someone devoid of talent —
I know more than most.

'Prince Urges the West to Learn from Islam'
(*The Times* headline 14. XII. 96)

Islam (that loudmouth jackass the Prince of
　　Wales has advised us)
offers alternative values to wicked
　　Westernist Science.
How many times does one have to reiterate
　　worldly Lucretius?:
Tantum religio potuit sua-
　　dere malorum.

Propertian (III. VIII)

What a wonderful row
  last night by candlelight!
What fine abuse spat
  from your lunatic lips
when, violent with wine,
  you kicked over the table
and viciously hurled
  your glass at my head!

Come on! Attack me!
  Rip out my hair!
Scar my face
  with your elegant nails!
Threaten to scorch
  my eyeballs out
with a brand from the fire!
  Wrench my shirt open,
tear it to tatters!

    There is no true love
without altercation –
  let *un*quarrelsome girls
be reserved alone
  for those I despise.

Let everyone look at
  my neck's raw love-bites;
let my contusions
  show I have been with you;
lend our love anguish –
  my tears or yours;
glower your admonishment;
  gesture obscenely.

I have no use
  for untroubled sleep.
Rage at me always
  while I wilt with pallor.

The last thing I want
  from *you* is a quiet life!

I.M., G.MacB.

Twenty-six years ago, sipping a Fino or
   two in the Langham,
      You and I spoke of the grave,
      also of Li Po *et al.*

How the departure of friends on a lengthy
   journey was somewhat
      similar to their demise –
      suddenly, they were not *here*.

How the convention of giving a willow wand
   to a departing
      friend who is travelling far
      features in much of Du Mu.

I said I thought it absurd to talk to the
   dead in a poem –
      death, *ipso facto*, precludes
      cosy perusal of verse.

      'Just a convention, of course,
      just a convention,' you said.

From the Chinese

Frost crisp in moonlight,
the delicate catkin trembles.

I bend a sprig and it snaps –
too late to present it to you!

Gula

'The scene here described with such vivid dramatic power took place, it is evident, in some large ale-house in London, not very far from Cock Lane, Smithfield, from Cheapside, and from Garlickhithe. It was also probably very near a church. It is a very curious fact, that there is absolutely no reason why the Boar's Head, in Eastcheap, immortalised by Shakespeare, should not have been the very tavern here meant…it boasted to be the "chief tavern in London", and (which is very curious) its back windows looked out on to the burial ground of St Michael's, a church which is now pulled down, but has given its name to St Michael's Lane.'

W.W. SKEAT, notes to PIERS THE PLOWMAN

Glutton was going . to get himself shriven,
and made for St Michael's . to confess his misdemeanours.
But Beton, of the Boar's Head, . bawled out 'Good morning!',
asked where was he walking to?, . what was he going for?
'To St Michael's,' he answered, . 'I mean to hear Mass –
I'll be shrived and shown . the shame of my sins.'
'But my beer is the best – . take a bench, drink a bellyful.'
Then Glutton goes in, . and a great gang after him:
Cicely (the shoemaker) . sat on the settle;
Watt (who keeps cattle) . called in with his wife;
Tim (the tinker) . and two of his trainees;
Hick (who hires horses) . and Hugh (who sells needles);
Clarice, of *Cock* Lane, . courting the clerk;
there were pickpockets; whores; . the hangman of Tyburn;
David (the ditch-digger) . with a dozen degenerates;
Sir Piers of Predie; . Pernell from Flanders;
a rebec fiddler; . a rogue; a felon;
a ratcatcher chap; . a Cheapside streetsweeper;
rope-makers; riding men; . Rosie the dish-seller;
Godfrey of Garlickhithe; . Griffith the Welsh;
it was teeming with tatters . by ten in the morning.
They gave Glutton good ale . to be going on with.

. . .

They were merry, morose, . and had many good drinking-songs,
and they sat there till evensong . singing in snatches,
till Glutton had gobbled . a good few gallons.
His guts started gurgling . like a grunting pigpen.

He pissed a potful . and proceeded thereafter
to blow like a bugle . out of his backside
till all who'd been awed . by his arsehole's musicianship
parried its perfume . by pinching their noses.
He couldn't stand still . or step out without his stick;
then he blundered about . like a blind busker's guide dog,
sometimes sideways . and sometimes reversing
(like the criss-cross course . of a catcher of birds
who lays lines in a maze . to enmesh his quarry).
His focus grew foggy . and failed at the doorway,
he staggered on the step . and dropped like a stone.
Clement (the cobbler) . caught him by the waist
to lift him and lay him . in his lap for a little;
but Glutton, ungrateful, . grimaced and groaned,
and puked up a pool . over the poor chap's pants –
not one cur in the county, . however clemmed,
would have guzzled that gruel . disgorged from his gullet,
so rank did it reek, . that rancid release.

Weeping and wailing, . his wife and his waif
humped him home . and helped him into bed.
His indulgence induced . great idleness in him,
so that he snored . through Saturday and Sunday;
sun waned, and he woke, . winked, wiped his eyes,
and his very first words were: . 'Where's the wassail-bowl?'
Again and again . his wife had a go at him
concerning the way . he had lived so wickedly,
until he was ashamed . and assailed by conscience,
and in crapulous remorse . he repented, praying:
'Oh God, I am Glutton, . and guilty of gourmandism –
overdoing it at dinner . and dallying over drink,
so that I've honked up . before I've gone half-a-mile,
and vomited victuals . that the poor would have valued.
I have feasted on fine fare, . even on fasting days.
I have tarried in taverns . to tope and to tittle-tattle.'
And in abject agony . he agreed to fast:
'Neither flesh nor fowl, . nor fish on a Friday,
shall sully my stomach . until such time
as Abstinence, my auntie, . allows its resumption
(though I've loathed the old hag . for as long as I've lived).'

Chatting to dead folk isn't my line at
  all (as you well knew);
    nevertheless, I now lapse
    (just a convention, of course):

Never again will I visit the Duke's Head,
  now you've quit Putney.
    Rather, pence jingling in hand,
    I (also) head for the pier.

Callimachan

Here Philip buried the youthful Nicoteles
  (died in his twelfth year)
    of whom his father was proud,
    for whom the future held hope.

Raphus cucullatus

Men call them *totersten* or *dod-aarsen;*
the whole crew made an ample meal from three,
and what remained was pickled for future use.

*

Walckvögel, being Dutch for 'disgusting bird',
men call them this; in colour they are grey;
they roam there in great plenty, insomuch
that daily the Dutch catch many and eat of them.
They capture the *Walckvögel* with their hands,
but are obliged to take good care these birds
do not attack them on the arms or legs,
their beaks being very strong and thick and hooked,
for they are wont to bite most desperate hard.

*

These *dronten, walyvogel* or *dottaerssen* –
even long boiling scarcely makes them tender,
but they remain tough, hard and leathery,
with the exception of the breast and belly,
which can be very good.

*

Five of our men
landed, provided with sticks, muskets, nets,
and sundry other necessaries for hunting.
They climbed up mountains, hills, and roamed through forests
and valleys, and in the three days they were out
they took a half a hundred *wallich-vogels*
which we then fetched on board, salted and ate.

*

There is a great bird, bigger than our swans,
with large heads, half of which is covered with skin
resembling a hood. These birds want wings,
in place of which are three or four dark quills.
The tail comprises slender, curved grey feathers.
We called them *Walgh-voghel*, for this good reason,
that the more we boiled them in gigantic vats,
the tougher and more uneatable they became.

*

This bird is more for wonder than for food,
though greasie stomaches may seek after them,
to the delicate of taste they are offensive
and of no nourishment. Men call 'em 'Doo-doo'.

En Attendant

I have been here now
for long enough to know that
you will not turn up.

Theognian [Theognis (*fl.* 530 BC)]

Futile to rail at the rasp of Privation, or
   sneer at a bankrupt –
      daily the scale dips or lifts;
      Zeus gives or else confiscates.

        *

Penury batters us, even the boldest,
   into submission,
      wrecks our resilience, hastes
      rheum and the white hair of age.

All you can do to escape is to drown or
   leap from a cliff face.
      Crushed by Privation you lose
      even the spirit to speak.

Nips

   Dreams, do not invoke
my dead love or I will wake
   filled with loneliness.

        *

   Loaves, baked fresh today,
fragrant at six this morning,
   stir my sense with scents.

[Untitled]

five-lane motorway/
five-mile tailback/
Council for the Preservation
of Urban Squalor/
Keep Death on the Roads/
ten-lane motorway/
Toyota to get us
back on our feet/
Council for the Preservation
of Rural Spoliation/
Council for the Spoliation
of All You Fuckers Out There/
The Grin Belt/
The Grim Belt/
Council for the Preservation
of the Council for the Preservation/
The Black Belt/
fifteen-lane motorway/
twenty-lane/
thirty/
forty/
– what the fuck
cover the fucking lot
with a fathom of fucking asphalt
and say bollocks to it

From the Chinese

I had been in Tsai Chin's army
for twenty-five years at war.
When I returned to my village
all was wrecked and weeds
prised through my floor, my wife
had deserted me long ago.
I drank wine and wept.

Catullan (CIII)

Do let me have back the dosh which I kindly
    lent to you last year,
        then, by all means, chatter on
        vapidly, as is your wont.

Or if you'd rather hang on to the money
    feel free to do so,
        then all I ask you is this:
        please shut your vacuous gob.

'Clear Beggars from Streets, says Blair'
(*The Times* headline 7. I. 97)

I want to clear the streets of beggars, vagrants
and people sleeping rough, and, furthermore,
clamp down on squeegee merchants loitering
at traffic lights to wash one's windscreen. Also,
I want graffiti artists put away.
I shall reclaim the streets from mendicants
and winos, addicts, people I don't like.
These 'homeless' can be downright threatening
and must be done away with – do you know,
I often drop my kids off at King's Cross
for them to take the Tube and, actually,
it's really quite a frightening place for people.
I think the basic principle is: Yes,
it's right to be intolerant of the homeless.
Do I give money to street beggars? No!
Occasionally I *do* buy *The Big Issue*,
so *that's* OK, but, really, it's appalling
that young people are sleeping in shop doorways.
So what I want is Zero Tolerance.

From the Chinese

I donate money to a beggar;
it is not much, but he has half my wealth.

I am reminded of the sage's words:
If the mendicant gets drunk tonight,
then I am happy also.

Salopian

All day, the drone of a saw,
and resin across the pines
of dark Mortimer Forest.
With each completed sever
it fell by a whining octave.

By dusk, in the clearing they'd made,
all that remained was their dust,
the dottle from someone's pipe
and ranks of seasoning limbs
weeping congealing amber.

                    *

The heat, the fragrance of hay,
the incontrovertible end
of summer, the country halt,
boarding the single-track train,
weeds prising the platform oblique
where they waved and waved and waved.

                    *

Dewed cowslips, roses, the grave
under a yew in the garden
of lichened Pipe Aston church,
a dusty Visitors' Book...

We were once there: 17th
of June 1975.

Obit

That old woman dead
in the downstairs apartment.
No more old-fangled
nether garments pegged outside
to offend our aesthetics.

[Untitled]

Inadequate lines
limited by syllables
charting lives, loves, deaths.

Tristia

Three times the river has frozen over.
Three times the black sea has frozen over.
Three years I have been here (it seems like ten)
where the solstices seem not to matter,
nights and days being the same to me (*long*);
where hostile people constantly threaten
rapine and summary execution;
where to venture out is to take great risk;
where living is flimsily established
and atrocities perpetuated;
where the smallholders are afraid to scrape
the stony dirt to achieve their pittance
(one hand ploughing, one clutching a weapon)
or tend their scruffy sheep while they listen
for the approach of hoofbeats and marching,
with nervous glances over their shoulders.

Theocritan (XXVII)

ACROTIME. Show me thy bountiful glade where thy sapling
growth is so rampant.

DAPHNIS. Come, then, and let me show thee my fast-growing
elegant cypress.

AC. Crop the grass, little goats, while I retire to
visit this neatherd.

DA. Guzzle, ye ravenous bulls, while I show this
delicate maiden
that which she wishes to see.

*

[Now the scene changes – herewith a stand of
   new-sprouted cypress.]

AC. Oh!, thou young satyr!, what art thou touching my
   breasts through my blouse for?

DA. First, I desire to test these velvety
   apples for ripeness.

AC. Dear God of Nature!, please do withdraw thy
   hand, for I feel faint.

DA. Courage, my sweet one, why shiver so? Art thou
   fearful or bashful?

AC. Why do'st thou topple me into a ditch, thus
   fouling my raiment?

DA. Notice, though, how that I give thee a gentle
   fur 'neath thy garment.

AC. Ah, me!, for thou hast ripped off my girdle!
   Why hast thou done so?

DA. This is my Paphian offering to sub-
   lime Aphrodite.

AC. Someone aproacheth!, I beg thee to stop this
   which thou art doing.

DA. 'Tis but the cypress, whispering at thy
   pure consummation.

AC. Oh!, thou hast torn all my underclothes off and
   now I am naked!

DA. I will now give thee a covering far more
   ample than they were...

[Untitled]

Bards write to the dead
'You were so this and so that' –
   corpses cannot read.
Mother and Father, *before*
you croak, I write to thank you.

OED

Two new words today,
each useless: *nimbiferous,*
   also *nidifice.*

Luger

During the Second World War
my father-in-law killed a German
from whom he stole a pistol.

When we collected his stuff,
after his stroke in the 'eighties,
we gave the gun in to Old Bill.

But I should have kept it, kept it
so that I could have, now,
blown my fucking brains out.

[Untitled]

Only in abject despair they glimpse the
    solace of Word-Hoard;
        then the bright casket's lid slams.
        sealing the treasure inside.

Propertian (IV. VII)

Ghosts *do* live;
   death doesn't end all:
the pale shade cheats
   the funeral pyre.

Over my bed
   Cynthia leaned,
though her ashes lay buried
   near the noisy highway.
Sleepless with grief
   after her obsequies
I lay lamenting
   in the sheets' bleak realm.

Her hair and her eyes
   seemed the same as they were
when she was borne
   on her bier at the end;
her charred dress
   adhered to her body;
the fire had melted
   her ring of beryl;
and although the bitter
   waters of Lethe
had scorched her lips
   she spoke in a voice
charged with living breath
   as her knuckles crackled
charcoal-brittle.

   'Treacherous lover!,
faithful to nobody,
   how can you sleep
at a time like this?
   Have you forgotten
the nights we made love
   breast to breast
till we warmed the bare street
   where we coupled and coupled

under our cloaks?
    Did anyone see you
prostrate with grief for me?,
    your mourning-clothes steaming
with tears of anguish?
    At least as far
as the gates, if you couldn't
    be bothered to go
any further, you could have
    asked my bearers
to walk more slowly,
    and lent the occasion
some semblance of dignity.

    And why were no fragrant
spices cast on my pyre?
    Was a bunch of cheap hyacinths
too much to ask of you?
    Could you not have breached
a bottle of wine
    and made a libation
to my spent spirit?
    But, though you deserve it,
Sextus Propertius,
    I shan't nag you now:
I know that for years
    your verses have honoured me.
May the adder hiss
    and writhe through my ribs
if I lie when I tell you
    that I have been faithful.

But now, if you're not
    besotted with Chloris,
hear what I wish:
    those poems you wrote to me,
burn them, burn them,
    make me no longer
an object of worship;
    clear from my grave
the virulent ivy
    which otherwise tangles
and twines round my bones;

incise in stone
  this noble epitaph
    that Romans may read it –
IN THE CLAY OF TIBUR
    CYNTHIA RESTS
ENDOWING GLORY
    TO ANIO'S BANKS.

And, Sextus, don't doubt
  apparitions that roam
from Elysian regions –
  such visions have weight.
By night we are free,
  unfettered shadows;
at dawn we are destined
  to turn back to Lethe
where Charon counts us
  carefully aboard.

Though others may have you now
  soon you'll be *mine*!
Together our bones
  will grind in union.'

Her indictment ended,
  I tried to embrace her,
but her shadow, like vapour,
  thinned, uncorporeal.

Distich

All that remained was to tidy the desk and
  type out the distich,
    then end the myth that they don't
    do it who *threaten* they will.

Ob.

(1999)

*(Those having precognition suffer
terror beforehand.)*

Meanings

With *sol.* it means scholastic disputation;
I'm told it means a tampon in the 'States;
a low half penny, such as you'd pay Charon;
the hapless git who waited for the quack.

Veracruz

Outside the village,
pellucid river
(*chicos*, splashing, squealed),
we were regaled with
kingfishers – Belted,
Green, Ringed, Amazon…

to celebrate which:
beer and salt and limes.

Coplas de Pie Quebrado

Wake, dull brain, and contemplate this:
how Death approaches silently;
   quick pleasure fails.

It is painful to remember
how, in the retrospect, the past
   was much better.

The present is gone in a flash,
and the future? Gone already.
   Expect nothing.

Lives? Rivers to the Sea of Death
where millionaires and mendicants
   perish the same.

I don't invoke religious bards –
their fictions stink of hog faeces,
   lie about Death.

This world only leads to the next,
but the journey is full of shit –
   birth, fucking, Death.

Even the Son of God came down
to get himself born on earth,
   then got murdered.

Lovely flesh cannot be remade;
in this impartial world we lose –
   age, disaster...

Tell me, how does beauty, pink flesh
and plump, opulent youthfulness
   end in old age?

The tricks, strength and agility,
physical prowess and power
   of youth soon die

when all turn to the dreariness
of Senility's grim suburb
   and zeal expires.

Who doubts that wealth and property
may at any time be taken?
   Fate's wheel spins fast.

This toilsome life's joys are short-lived;
we rush headlong into Death's snare;
   no turning back.

Popes, emperors, prelates, pig-herds
fetch up the same; even great kings
   run out of luck.

Ubi sunt Romans, Greeks, Trojans?
King Don Juan? Aragon's princes?
   All those gallants?

Their numerous innovations?
Jousts, embroideries, ornaments?
   Proud heraldry?

Were they mere imagination?
Merely chaff on the threshing-floor
   after harvest?

What has become of the women,
their dresses, their scents, their coiffures,
   their love affairs?

The flames of the fires they kindled?
The dulcet music, the dancing,
   the wines, the mirth?

The regal palace treasuries,
the resplendent goblets, the gold,
   steeds, harnesses?

Mere dew of the morning meadows,
mere dew of the morning meadows,
    mere dew, mere dew...

Dukes, marquises, counts, warriors –
where have you delivered them, Death,
    in your mad rage?

The pennants, banners, standards, flags,
unassailable castles, walls,
    ramparts, bulwarks,

barricades, ditches, refuges...
of what use, of what use, of what
    use, of what use?

51st

As each sidereal spin
   impartially hurtles us on
towards yet another birthday
   and extirpation at last,
three consolations at least:
   verse; viticulture; love.

Chiricahuas, Arizona,

four-and-a-half mile ascent
through resinous pines to the crest's
defunct fire lookout cabin
perched on a crag at 9,000

where a tiny alpine meadow
(burgeoning moist crisp verdure
and carmine blooms distilling
nectareous fumes, and a single
Rufous Hummingbird)
was suddenly epiphanic.

Workshop

You say you *love* words?
Hmmm, let me see: 'Sweet zephyr...';
    keep up the good work.

Flyer

...poetry reading...rare opportunity...
one of the leading...whose reputation is...
    recent collections: *Foibles*, *Frog's Breath*...
    gained international...lyric beauty...

At the Reading

The sham-coy simper,
the complacency,
the *frisson* titters,
the sycophancy.

In the SCR

The puerile academic quips,
the smugly learnèd repartee
withstanding little scrutiny.

Catullan

Possibly I may find time to peruse your
   puerile outpourings
      (I don't remember your name);
      more likely, though, I shall not.

[Untitled]

   Unfortunately
an A in Histrionics
   doesn't count for much.

Veracruz

A dirt road furrowed and flooded,
a brown sow truffling the verge.
We thought it a tin-roofed pig-pen
with one wall down and the floor
ankle deep in hog shit,
until we saw through the fug
of its furthest corner a gleam
of embers and, blowing the charcoal
alive, a woman cooking
tortillas and black beans and chilli.

*

A rickety table on which
surf from the *Bahía* slapped
whenever a big wave creamed
over the rocks that supported
the bar, Brown Pelicans
crumpling into the foam,
a Magnificent Frigatebird
in the Zeiss in the gathering gloom,
to celebrate which we ordered
more beer and salt and limes.

*

Montezuma Oropendolas
glug-glugged like bottles emptied
where the boss on a Palamino
drew from an ornate machete sheath
a flashy blade and proceeded
to slash at a bunch of bananas
proffered by lachrymose labourers
lining the dirt road where
Montezuma Oropendolas
glug-glugged like bottles emptied.

Recollection

When you playfully
locked the door and dropped the key
    between your huge breasts.

Mnemonic

Whenever I whiff
Pont l'Evêque I recollect
    your cunt, Carolyn.

At Chesapeake Bay

When we arrived at the stubble fields dawn hadn't
  lit the horizon.

As a glim sun rose up grudgingly, suddenly,
  out of puce cirrus,

skein after skein after skein after skein after
  skein after skein of

Canadas yonking in spirals of downpouring
  thousands and thousands

onto the frost-solid gleaning-grounds. Half-an-hour
  later the land was

darkened in front of us, thick with the *Brantas* and
  Brantas and – wait, though;

one single *Chen caerulescens*, pure white
  Snow in the black mass.

Fumbling fingers focused the Zeiss, homed
  in on the... Well it

wasn't Divine Revelation, I know, but the
  one thing I think of,
    think of again and again
    now, in the oxygen tent.

Shropshire Lads

('*Clear Beggars from Streets, says Blair*'
– The Times *headline 7.i.97*)

When supermarkets open at 8 a.m.
the lads nick double litres of Scrumpy Jack,
the lads who, hourly, try the Returned Coins slots
of phone boxes which stink of piss and fags.
Oh yes, even in Salop. they are there,
anathemas of Tony fucking Blair.

[Untitled]

A reach of Severn such as Elgar knew,
redolent of Englishness and English art;
a boathouse with a plaque incised *I.M.*
LIEUTENANT LESLIE SHAW WHO COACHED THE EIGHTS...
the kind of Englishman who went, when called,
with decency, and who did not come back.

Veracruz

October morning in Cardel, roof of the Hotel Bienvenido in great heat and with no shade. As thermals form, kettles of Broad-Winged and Swainson's Hawks and Turkey Vultures boil up circling to a thousand feet above the coastal corridor, stream south on the currents until dwindling to infinity in the Zeiss. With the raptors, Anhingas, Wood Storks, White Pelicans. For three hours migration is continuous, three hundred thousand birds, then nothing. We, also, depart, and no poem can adequately celebrate this generous transience.

[Untitled]

In this Stygian city
a machine vends fruity condoms
(strawberry, lemon 'n' lime),
a confectioner's glowing window
displays a chocolate rat.

Nocturne

The fulminant dusk,
the price of petrol,
the cost of living,
the mute finale
molto allegro

[Untitled]

Shostakovich 5's
manic pretence of
zealous applause for
the trampling march of
Uncle Joe's heavies.

?

Soon and silently,   in a dark suit...
Men at the mead-bench,   meditate, name him.

Chinoiserie

(Deborah: ten   thousand sighs;
ten thousand nights'   golden wine!)

Cold light   on my floor
mimics   frosty ground.

Look up,   see the moon!
Cowed, I   think of home.

I drink   wine and drowse,
petals   fall on me.

Sober: what remains?
Few friends,   me, the moon.

Where's it from, that   mellow flute
borne on the spring   midnight wind,

pervading all   this mute town
with remembered   tunes from youth?

Dusk: I scramble   from the heights.
Under full moon   I leave tracks
blue in snow. You   welcome me,
lead me on to   your snug shack.

Children guide us   through bamboo
by a footpath   hung with vines
to this welcome   resting place
where you pour me   well made wine.

Pine trees sigh while   we carouse
through the night till   stars have waned.

Drunkenly we   have achieved
severance from   worldly cares.

Vintner (now   where eternal
rivers run),   do you still stock
that prime cru   *Agèd Springtime*?

If you do,   who buys it, since
I can't (yet)   visit your realm?

Mountain flowers   bloom, we drink:
wine, and more wine,   wine again...

I am drunk; go,   while I sleep.
Return at dawn,   bring your lyre.

A lovely girl   furls the blind.
Her brows flutter   as she sits.

Who is the cause   of her grief?
Only tearstains   indicate.

Each day   of the year
I drink   till I slump.

Though you   married me
any   sot would do.

Handsome, young,   a horseman comes;
blossom falls,   hooves trample it.

Now his whip   scrapes the panel
of a fine   carriage passing.

The ornate   curtain twitches,
she inside   is beautiful –

'I live there'   she whispers, smiles,
indicates   a small pink house.

Here's wine   tinted gold;
once more   fill my glass.

See its   amber gleam!
Scent its   fumous depths!

Only   get me drunk,
landlord,   then I'll feel

no more   homesickness
in this   foreign place.

Parted,   I lament.
Chill moon   lights my house.

Still no   letter comes.
I see   geese fly north;

I see   geese fly south.
Still no   letter comes.

Don't let gold wine,   in its cask
under the moon,   lie alone.

Exiled, I came   drifting here.
Hazy distance   hides my home.

Now, a mellow   bamboo flute –
'Falling Blossoms'   is the air.

Ravaged now, the   lavish park;
weeds prise crumbled   walls apart;
sad notes issue   from songbirds.

Only the moon   is constant,
shining above   the ruin
as it shone once   on noble
guests at Fu Chai's   great palace.

Just to   fan myself
too much   work, I let

wind through   forest pines
cool my   bare body.

Lake and egrets   in moonlight.
Do you hear that?   Girls' voices –

water-chestnut   gatherers
go home tonight   in sweet song.

She plucks lilies   from the Yeh.
A man passes,   her boat turns.

In the lotus   she hides, laughs,
coyly pretends   not to look.

You ask to know   my sorrow –
when spring ends watch   petals drop!

I would tell you   but speech fails.
I sign and seal   this letter,

a thousand miles   I send it,
remembering   forever.

A girl   on the bank,
a man   in his boat,

exchange   fond glances,
depart   heartbroken.

Reflux   of the tide.

He has   now returned,
from his   exile, home.

Tears fall,   lucid pearls.

Let us purchase   wine today –
do not say the   cost is high.

Sell my horse and   my fine coat,
then, with good wine,   you and I

will forget ten   thousand years
of deep sorrows   and be cheered!

From bamboo screens   young girls glide,
silk robes lifting   as they dance.

One man's   silent bones...
I sigh   to look back,

I sigh   to go on.
What goal   keeps us here?

                    Autumn wind
                is chill, the moon full,
            leaves scutter, crows quit cold roosts.
        This night, this hour, your absence, love's ache.

A hundred jars   we despatched
to flush sorrow   from our hearts.

Such junketing   by moonlight –
no one desired   sleep that night.

But, drunk at last,   down we lay,
sky for blanket,   earth for bed.

Golden wine in   golden cups…
We were soon joined   by a girl
(eyebrows painted,   slippers pink)
who beguiled us   when she sang.

As we feasted   so we drank
till she rested   in my lap –
what cavortings   we then had,
curtained from the   revellers!

Why labour?   Life is to dream.
Today's wine   has made me doze,
my back propped   against the door.

I wake up: what month is this?
Trees blossom   out of focus,
a bird sings   on the spring breeze.

Morose now,   I pour more wine
and sing while   the moon rises.

My song ends,   I pour more wine –
my sorrow?,   unremembered.

Three years   since you left,
perfume   lingers still.

I sigh –   sered leaves fall;
weep – dew   glints on moss.

In her   loveliness
she is   like a bloom –

scented   peony
rich with   honeydew.

Southern girls have   lucent skin,
flirtatious spring   in their eyes.

They pick lilies   from the lake,
smile, hand them to   passing men.

Flickering lamp,   the cold moon;
we are drinking   heavily.

Our ribald din   flushes out
a white egret   from the reeds.

So soon, it seems,   midnight comes.

From the open   window, sky;
when the moon rose   we drank more.

Banished, I climb   this high place,
remember home.   The year's end:

the sun setting,   water, cloud,
the mountain pines,   geese in flight,

the horizon   growing dark.

Gongs, drums,   dainty foods –
all of   little worth.

Only   joyful wine –
drain ten   thousand cups!

This night   Mirror Lake
shines bright   in the moon.

A girl's   reflection
shivers –   quicksilver!

I complain –   Alas, mirror:

hair of jet   in the morning;
driven snow   by the evening.

While we may,   take our pleasure.

How gaunt   you've become!
Are you   suffering?

Is it   Terminal
Acute   Poetry?

Do not   hesitate –
spend your   wealth on wine.

Slay the   calf and lamb,
drink three   hundred cups!

In the Pleasure   Palaces
they would feast, in   bygone times,

with ten thousand   cups of wine
and carouse with   carelessness.

Then Han-chung's   great Governor
rose and danced,   completely drunk.

Decked in his   official robes
I, drunk too,   fell in a heap,

chose his lap   to rest my head,
went to sleep   until moonrise.

Singing-girls,   their faces rouged,
drunk, turn to   the setting sun.

Journeyed on,   came to Pe-liang,
many months –   what revelry!

How much gold   we squandered then!

Cups of jade,   sumptuous food,
wine in huge   extravagance!

Crows croak   to their roosts.
This girl   at her loom,
for whom   does she weave,
mumbling   to herself?

She thinks   of a man
many   miles away.
She must   sleep alone.
Her tears   like drizzle.

In obscure streams   lotus grows,
beautiful in   morning sun.

No one knows, though,   of its worth,
its rare perfume.   Frost is due –
colour will fade,   scent diffuse.

Better if it   were rooted
here in this safe   garden pool.

By sea,   Chao, you left
to view   fabled lands.

But now   the moon sinks,
grey clouds   fill the sky.

Green spring, but I   grow white-haired
on this bank of   the Yangtze.

My shadow here,   thoughts elsewhere,
my poor garden   choked with weeds.

What to do so   late in life
but sing my songs   and forget?

Kites and ravens   feast on guts;
generals gain   not one thing.

Poverty strikes!   In sorrow
I consume two   thousand jugs,
until, at last,   spring returns.

You are so wise –   you prefer
to constantly   remain drunk
and travel by   modest mule.

Spring wind ripples   our gold wine
but soon dies down.   Petals fall.

Beautiful girl,   blushed with drink,
how long do peach   and plum bloom?

Transient light   tricks mankind;
tottering age   soon arrives.

The sun moves west,   arise, dance!
Silver silk hair   soon enough.

Copla de Pie Quebrado

Consolatory tears, flow, flow
and wet my cheeks as usual:
    love kills us all.

Everglades

Hundreds of pounds per square inch
of grinning gator's jawbones
crunching a two-foot catfish.

That *leisurely* crackling
recurs in thrilling nightmares.

Nocturne

Melancholy   striking me,
I imbibed wine   to excess.

Temporary   respite came,
counterfeit and   shallow mirth.

But tonight the   void returns,
there is no sleep,   misery,

worries (fiscal   and of death),
fear and abject   black despair.

Veracruz

A colony of Howler Monkeys,
enraged by sudden tropical rain,
grumbling *pp* from the canopy,
swelling to bloodcurdling *fff*;

a hand-sized tarantula groping its route
between puddles across the flooded dirt road;

a Laughing Falcon (plate 3
in Peterson's *Field Guide to Mexican Birds*),
black facial mask, cream/buff crown and underparts,
perched preening after the deluge
ten metres distant in perfect visibility.

At the first bar, beer and limes
to honour these grave occurrences.

Little Ones

(I.M., G.E.)

National Geographic

Vast tracts of shit have yet to be discovered.

Miltonic

They also serve who only stand and wank.

Found

These sleeping tablets may cause drowsiness.

Melancholic

'No man amongst us so sound, of so good a constitution, that hath not some impediment of body or mind ... All this befalls him in this life, and peradventure eternal misery in the life to come.'
ROBERT BURTON, The Anatomy of Melancholy

I know not whence he came, but a wise man
had a coarse, strident termagant of a wife;
and when she brawled, he played upon his drum,
and by that means he maddened her the more,
because she saw that he would not be vexed.

*

All black wines, over hot, compounded, strong,
thick drinks as malmsey, alicant, brown bastard,
muscadine, rumney, metheglin, and such,
of which they have, in Muscovy, a plenty,
are hurtful to the melancholic head,
for wine itself causeth that very ill,
especially if immoderately imbibed.

Guianerius tells a story of two Dutchmen,
to whom he gave the freedom of his house,
'that in one month's space both were melancholy
by drinking wine – the one did naught but sing,
the other sigh.'

*

Unholy desperation,
says Tully, is a sickness of the soul
with neither hope nor any expectation
of succour; for whilst evil is *expected*,
we fear; but when 'tis *certain*, we despair.

Everglades

Roseate Spoonbills
against a florid sunset,
    transcending sunset...
[Balderdash: Nature Poems
(*all* poems) – inadequate.]

Coplas de Pie Quebrado

*Own*ing! *Own*ing! *Own*ing! *Own*ing!
Kill them cruds who rob yr. limo!
 ¡*Viva* death squads!

Torture, waste delinquent assholes!
When I lived in Buenos Aires
 I killed two kids –

what the hell!?, they stole some CDs
out of *my* car (*any*one would
 shoot them mothers).

We killed more than forty minors
in them slums in Guatemala –
 they deserved it.

They was trash, them beggars, robbers,
garbage-gleaners, truly assholes.
 So we trashed them –

gouged their eyes out, hacked their ears off,
cut their tongues out, left them fester
 in the trash dump.

Don't forget: the right to *own* is
high priority; the right to
 live is *nada*.

Medieval

A joyful time,
while summer lasted,
with birds' singing...

But now, gales gust,
sleet slashes,
night is never-ending,

and I, remorseful,
am melancholic,
mourn and clem myself.

Axiomatic

Man, who seldom lives a hundred years,
worries himself enough for a thousand.

*

Small-talk will charm a host;
straight-talk provokes dislike.

*

Better to die ten years early
than spend those extra years in penury.

*

I do not laugh at this old fart,
for I shall assuredly be thus.

*

Old and yellow men,
and pearls when they are yellow, are
equally worthless.

*

Each birthday one knows
next year will be worse.

*

Though we so vividly dream
of our boyhood games, our cruel mirrors
reflect snow-haired old codgers.

The New Book

Small and dangerous,
like a *sgian dubh*.

Nouvelle Cuisine

...and to follow:
jellied tripes, flung
on a fresh bed
of whimsical
Cajun hogsnot.

Ob.

That last   journeying
in pain   and in fear.

Stone

Where *gravitas* nor levity can stir him.

MARFAN

(2000)

Look eastward from the back porch in late June:

Venus ascends, one hour before the Sun,
over the water tower (which fecund belly
sustains this drouth-town's viability).

'Aint none knows whar she come from, o whar shays goin.'

'Jus rides that *burro* roun from place to place.'

'Ya sees her whan yer least expectin it...'

The Burro Lady ties her moke to a post
at Chuy's (now defunct) Mexican Diner
and goes for coffee into Dairy Queen.

She has the *frisson*-fright air of a gypsy –
gaudily-coloured wrap-rounds, plastic flip-flops
with spurs incongruously fixed at the heels.

The *burro*, draped with saddle-bags and blankets,
is pale, pale, pale, pale, in this evening's light.

I don't know what they signify, but it's scary.

Reading in Marfa Public Library:
Qui Caecus et Senectute Confectus.

Across an arid, silent scrubland blackness
the raucous trumpet hails the malfortunates...

Night, Union Pacific freight trains braying
lullaby them to sleep: ˘ — | ˘ —

Approaching D (*allegro moderato*).

One evening, back in 1883,
Robert Reed Ellison was with his wife
herding a bunch of cattle across the basin
from Alpine towards Marfa, heading west,
and, sundown coming on, stopped for the night.
As he made preparations for the campfire
he glanced up and was mystified to notice
lights flickering to and fro across a valley
along the side of the Chinati Mountains.
Assuming it was Apaches on the move,
he catnapped clutching his Winchester till dawn
when the weird incandescence fizzled out.

A short time after that, a young surveyor,
man by the name of Williams, was out mapping
round the same spot and saw the same strange lights.
His journal records how 'Indians of this region
believe the luminosity to be
the restless spirit of the dead Apache,
Chief Alsate.'

          Nearly a century later,
the *Houston Chronicle* despatched Stan Redding –
'Check out this Marfa story; let's just see
whether there's anything in it.' As he drove

along a dirt road near Paisano Pass,
Redding observed the Marfa Mystery Lights:
They darted about the ground – red, white and blue,
orbs, baseball-sized. They blended into one,
then separated. One of them would zoom
high in the air, then plummet into the brush,
then rise an instant later and spin away
crazily. Unsupported and unattached,
each one illuminated the black-brush clump
over which it hovered.

Tonight, off 90 East,
a curious *ignis fatuus* fulminates...

[Some feller driving a Chevrolet pickup truck
gave me a ride from Alpine on East 90,
and, as we motored, confided this to me:]

Ya know, thay stop me sometimes, tham thar cops,
*and take me downtown with'm tew thar **station**.*
*Thay thay thay thay thay make me do tham **tests**.*
*Thay say ah done a **wrong thang**, but ah never.*
*Thay say mah wrists got someways sort of **gashed**.*
*Thay say people like me is goddam **pests**.*
Thay thay thay thay thay found me in a drain
*and sent me to that **Rehabilitation***
***Center** (that's whar thay send ya whan ya **trashed**),*
thay gev ya coffee thar and feed ya slops...

[Then let you out to *integrate* again
and makeshift to the best of your endeavour.]

The dress and souvenir shop on the corner
was formerly Kerrs' Filling Station – back
in 1920, Arthur, Orr and Klyde
Kerr purveyed Fords, served gas and were mechanics
for the few cars in Marfa, and they supplied
kerosene for folks' lamps.

                        The brothers Kerr
sold W.H. Cleveland, a local rancher,
a Model T. They showed him how to start it,
which process Cleveland grasped, but they neglected
to demonstrate how he should stop the thing.

He scorched off to his ranch, yelled the day's orders
to his cowhands, U-turned and headed back
to Marfa.

                Circling round and round and round
in front of Kerrs' he hollered '*WHOA THAR, HOSS!*'
repeatedly until one of the brothers
leapt on the running-board, roped in the critter,
and skidded it adroitly to submission
swathed in a cloud of Southwest Texas dust.

The depositional Marfa Basin formed
during the Permian (which began about

280,000,000 years ago
and lasted about 55,000,000 years) –
a shallow, bowl-like sea where sediments
accumulated (and where we now walk,
perpetuating the depositional trait).

A Union Pacific freight train hurtles
through the night town; at each street intersection
(bells, red lights, semaphore of barber-pole
barriers) the engineer hits the hooter –
a raucous howl, audible for five miles
across the silent, arid scrubland basin
where, in a blackness, some malfortunate
is woken by the cacophonic trumpet,
listens, and ruminates, and fears the dark.

Tonight's anxieties: a labial lump;
pain in the kidneys and the abdomen;
and money, money, money, money, money.

where maledicts are shivering in the pit
though scorching heat is unassuaged   where breath
exhaled is woeful   where black corvids scavenge

A solitary, voluntary exile
respires hot, fan-rotated desert air
in a southwestern public library.

where they lie sullen in black slurry   where
powerless to speak they gurgle disregarded
where dolorous groans begin   where plangent wails
of lamentation sickeningly arise
where no light penetrates   where Stygian squalls
thrash every victim equal   desperate shrieks
and supplicant imprecations are ignored

The final over; everyone is out.

The Classics shelf in Marfa Public Library:
incongruously stuffed between two volumes
of the *Commedia*, a tattered *Wisden*
charts the achievements of that English summer
before climacteric and post bellum slump.

The Mourning Dove bag should be good round Marfa;
meanwhile, the telly chirpily reports
it's Open Season on the kids in Baghdad.

Wine from Fort Stockton; sunset; Chinese poem.

I blow the Chihuahuan dust from his *Collected*.
Ewart is three-years-dead; this is the desert.

A roadside Turkey Vulture scrutinises
the hesitant progress of a passer-by.

The First Episcopal Church of Holy Shit
clanks its complacent bell across the basin.

Even the *Big Bend Sentinel*, each week
conveys them mercilessly down the Rio –
Hernandez, Martinez, Garcia, Lopez...

We are applying *Nature's Miracle*
unto the furnishings we have besmirched.

Fuentes, Vega, Valverde, Rivera,
Morales, Flores, *descanse en paz.*

Beyond my caring and my comprehension.

We term it Marfa, but we mean the lot.

Across the windswept, Pronghorn-browsed brown grass
Judd's row of concrete, seven-foot-high boxes
stretches a mile north-south, signifies zilch.

Some days I've seen *Antilocapras* shelter
from noon sun of a hundred-and-some degrees
in those cute sculptures – yes, and shit in'm too.

Last night the snow began. At 4 this morning
the flakes are flinty, seem to shrink the face.
The walk down Washington from North Plateau –
2 inches of parochial Amundsen.

A fellow Lone Star drinker in Ray's Bar:
'Whan ya git old ya can't remember a fuck.'

Look west, beyond the Mexican Cemetery,
the Rothko Sunset and oblivion.

A CD, placed incongrously in Marfa:
Georg Philipp Telemann, who understood,
among so many other important issues,
the order of obeying descending scales.

The Baptists are in confident full cry –
their happy howls and yelps sweal from the window
of a charming little breeze-block tabernacle
and rise to join the welter of emissions
from the industrial plants both sides the border
conspiring to occlude the clear-sightedness
of those who live in Big Bend.

                              Crossing 90,
observe, above the Thunderbird Motel,
how all the shit belched skywards contributes
to the beauty of this monumental Sunset.

El Paso Airport, the Departure Lounge,
beyond the Baggage Check, beyond the Gate,
beyond the Terminal and the Rio Grande,
Mark Rothko strata grade from blood to black.

Sunset is like a busted-up fried egg.

No; like an addled egg, with drops of *sangre*.

'We love it here!', expressive of ennui.

The last ebb, the dead shingle – Marfa Basin.

The Wisdom of West Texas, a slim vol.

When this gets published I shall have to be
beyond the City Limit on a Greyhound.

For I am catapulted to the grandeur
of Marfan Literary Resident
(sinecure recently inaugurated
by the beneficence of Patrick Lannan –
blessandpreservehimandhiswholeFoundation).

Their countree doe poffefs an myriad temples:
Papifts, Epifcopalians, Methodifts,
Cowboys for Chrift, and ye Jehovah's Witnefs…
Truly a fere, yet pious, wildernefs.

The ftimulus of ftrong drink is oft required.

'Twas then they sent in Lannan's Secret Weapon.

From the Mexican: The Sun unfoldeth pink
on peaks across the Rio Bravo – ridge
on ridge on ridge on ridge on ridge on ridge...
and I am exiled in El Paso Airport
while my belovèd flyeth; yet the Sun
riseth, illuminateth – is this hope?

The artist Donald Judd deigned to descend
here in the 1970s, and proceeded
(courtesy of vast funding from his patron)
to launch himself indulgently upon
a spoilt-child, hedonistic shopping-spree
procuring half the town.

               In '79,
to gratify a yen to establish plush
permanent installations of his own
and of his buddies' bourgeois artefacts,
he bought the army camp, or, as he writes
with characteristic magnanimity
and not a little chutzpah: 'I agreed
to have the Dia Foundation come to Marfa
and purchase the main buildings and the land
of Fort D.A. Russell, on the edge of town.'

That's where he housed his famous magnum opus –
one hundred waist-high milled aluminium boxes
betokening genius spawned of privilege.

Manifestly possessed of major talent,
what ingenious *kunstwerke* would he have, perforce,
produced if big-money backers had been absent
to finance these billion-dollar, minimalist,
factory-finish, self-indulgent art games?

In Judd's *Collected Writins* he says, I'm tole:
'I have a complex on a city block
in Marfa, Texas, between Highway 90
and the Southern Pacific Railroad Company track
next to a cattlefeed mill, *unfortunately*' –
he'd bought the place in the early '70s
an found he couldn't git tew sleep o'nights
because of th'honest noise of manufacture.

Now Godbold's mill was established back in May
of 1946 when 'Happy' Roy Godbold
bought the feed business off'n ol' Harper Rawlings –
the name thay gev it wus 'Ranchers' Feed & Supplies'.
Seems to me carpetbaggers shouldn't complain.

The Marfan Bourgeois with their *Howdy, Peter!*s...
After about a dozen Margaritas
I puke and say how cute their 3-piece suite is.

[The Chevy driver is on red alert:]

Ya know thay got this television disc
outside mah neighbor's cabin but thay don't know
ah know it's not for satellite TV
but that thay got it pointing right inside
mah head the CIA tew find out what
ah think about tham beamed encrypted signals
transmitted from the Godbold's feedmill silo
beaming mah brains up tew the President
who sent the US Navy into town
tew place electric wiring between me
and the Presidio County Courthouse statue
which prickly pears transmits it tew the White House
out of the desert whan the Pentagon
will tell me that that that the President
that that that that that handgun that that that

Presidio County Courthouse, Marfa, built
in 1886 of native stone
and bricks made locally, three storeys high
with an octagonal tower capped by a dome
on top of which the fancy classical figure
of Justice once held in her outstretched digits
the symbol of her calling but now fingers
only the dusty hot air off the desert –
an irate cowpoke back in history,
quitting the calaboose across the street
(where he'd been held for being drunk), observed
'There *ain't* no justice in this goddam county',
and shot the scales plumb out of the goddess's hand.

Stone calaboose, built 1886
but now redundant, used for archiving
paperwork from the County Sheriff's office;

foot-thick steel door; a steel-grilled fenestration;
torn scribbled notice **JAiLeR WiLL HAnd oUT rAZORs
To gET A rAZEr YoU MUSt HAnD OnE iN**;

the 'Old Cage' dumped nostalgically out front,
incorporating four fold-down steel bunks
within the cramped cold ferric lattice trap.

To the Editor, the *Big Bend Sentinel* –
Sir, I was on 90, Marfa to Alpine,
when a white sport utility vehicle came
right up behind and passed me pretty quick.

My Cruise Control was set at 70
(the legal limit in Presidio County).

I couldn't help but notice that on the rear
license plate was inscribed the following
in fancy letters: **Texas County Judge**.

Ah holed up with a bunch of Peccaries
[*Tayassu tajacu*], tham Javelinas.

Ah'd fell out with the wife an drank some Lone Stars,
than, thar in that Fort D.A. Russell outfit,
ya know, whar thay got all tham Artist Judds?,
ah seen em headin into the ventilation
gap of a beat-up hut as ain't been touched
since 1946 or tharabouts.

Wall, what'd ah do but foller em right in thar –
a big ol' boar about a meter long,
four females an a couple o' young uns, yaller,
with black stripes down thar backs, an thar thay lay.

O' course the ol' male grunted an barked a whiles,
but ah jus crep thar, mong the shit an cobwebs,
an soon thay all jus fell asleep – it's hot, see?,
bout over a hundred in the middle day
(normly, thay'd be in Prickly Pear or brush).

Wall, ah wus thar for bout two hours, an than
thay high-tailed, doin Peccary stuff, ah guess.

The *fons et origo*, El Cheapo Liquor,
good Mescal with its fat worm in the lees,
Agave, armed with teeth like a goddam shark.

It's Xenophobia, but pretends to be
outraged concern that hundreds of tons of drugs
are flooding across the Mexico/US line
each year – the hatred's in the stupid faces,
the stupid quasi-military duds,
the stupid guns of off-duty Patrolmen
in Carmen's stuffing their porcine guts with shite
before resuming the cat-and-mouse charade
of rounding up the smooth-faced, terrified *hijos,*
viejas, campesinos cowered in scrub
this side the Rio Grande...

Washington:
congressional Republicans are baying
for bigger fences, more technology,
more agents and the US military
to stem the tide; the House of Representatives
is calling for 10,000 soldiers to guard
2,000 miles of US/Mexican frontier,
elaborate triple-fencing barriers
(*especially whar tham mothers tries to crass*
from Juárez to El Paso), and an entire
new agency for borderline enforcement
(*our border's a national secur'ty threat,*
and bah God, sah!, bah God, sah!, Congress better
start a-securin-of our border, pronto!).
The Senate is considering these demands
together with one to add 5,000 more
Border Patrol Gestapo and to provide
sophisticated high-tech apparatus
for the fat, trigger-happy, complacent twats.

Wash Your Hands

...ed in border
shooting of teen-age boy

13.viii.98 Biefend Sadin E.M.

Sixteen new Border Patrol recruits were sworn in Monday as the agency increases its presence here.

Peter Reading
2.ix.98.

116

[The Mystery Lights, the *ignis fatuus*
that hurteth not, but only feareth fooles,
elucidated by the Chevy driver:]

Ya know, tham lights back thar on 90 East,
thays flickerin signal messages tew me
most every night straight from the CIA,
thay thay thay thay thay thay thay thay thay thay
thay say thay say   ah keep mah handgun loaded

In January 1881,
work on the Galveston/San Antonio
Southern Pacific Railroads reached this site,
a water stop and freight headquarters which, then,
had no name. Southern Pacific's Engineer
was married to a woman who aspired
to *higher things* (was reading Dostoevski,
The Brothers Karamazov, 1880);
she dubbed the tank town Marfa, after the loyal
retainer of the Karamazov household,
omniscient old Marfa Ignatyevna
who did not see the fall but heard the scream,
the strange, foam-stifled, long familiar scream
of an epileptic falling in a fit.

The Lights, demystified by divers eminents:
electrostatic discharge; swamp-gas; moonlight
shining on veins of mica; ghosts of Spanish

Conquistadors who sought gold here; a mirage
produced by cold and hot layers of air
refracting light; *Ya know tham Mystery Flickers?,*
well, what it is, the CIA is beaming
encrypted messages from Washington
onto the water tower – ya know, that silver
cylinder thar with MARFA writ on?, well,
tham coded signals bounce right off the tower
and light up the entire Chinati Mountains
with flicker flicker flicker flicker flicker

US 90 East, Marfa to Alpine:
you drive through the volcano of Paisano –
just breccia 35 million years old,
caldera, and pale rhyolite, and you.

No-nuke groups lobby governor to resist
proposals for Sierra Blanca site.
(Headline in this week's *Big Bend Sentinel*.)

Sierra Blanca residents have voiced
concern over the Texas, Maine and Vermont
Compact, which would enable the three states
to dump low-level radioactive shit
on an impoverished minority's doorstep,
in violation of the federal
and international environmental
agreements made between the USA
and Mexico.

It doesn't matter though –
they're only Spiks out on the borderline
(a site beneath which lie tectonic faults
rendering it more seismically active
than any other in the Lone Star State).

Outside the Mexican Cemetery, a sign
to visitors is crackling and buckled
from solar blistering over generations
and winds sand-blasted off the Chihuahuan Desert:
$200 FINE FOR LOITERING
OR LITTERING HERE.

                    In this place idlers throng;
discarded stones, wood crosses, painted plaster,
and plastic roses faded to pinkish grey
garbage the quiet, death-sustaining slope.

Morales, Marquez, Garcia, Martinez,
Flores, Rivera, Hinojos-Hernandez...

Spiked on a Yucca sprouting from the dirt
of Maria Bartolo Villanueva,
a straw-stuffed rag doll, smiling, rosy-cheeked,
sporting a hat of bean-sack hessian –
the pious tribute of some *hijo*.

                    Coveys
of Scaled Quail loiter, litter among the ash,
scutter a dusty plot where Moniga
Quinteros de Salgado is reposing,
churr a low nasal *Descanse en Paz*.

The bails are scattered, the last man run out.

Wisden recalls the English ignominy…
A solitary, voluntary exile
respires hot, fan-rotated desert air
in a southwestern public library.

$10 in advance! The Marfa Lights
Festival (held on Labor Day Weekend)!
This year we feature the great Dana Lee
& Mariachi de la Paz of Alpine;
the one and only Shelly Lares – enjoy!
[Also, a bunch of other total shites
like 'Randy' Bob Pulido ('Texas Cowboy');
and, all the way from Marfa, 'Injun Dancers';
'Los City Boyz'…] **And, don't forget, at 9,**
the 3-on-3 Hoop-D-Do Street Basketball
Tournament – remember, y'all come and see…
[some banjo-pluckin' strumpet from Big Bend –
all in all, a load of fucking chancers.]
Way wish a Texas 'Howdy!' tew y'all!

The Editor, the *Big Bend Sentinel* – Sir,
Miguel de la Madrid and Ronald Reagan
agreed the Treaty of 1983,
protecting a zone 60 miles either side
the US/Mexico border, and committing
each government to turn down any project
that could affect the other's side of the line.

In 1998 the US House
of Representatives agreed a measure
allowing Maine and Vermont to ship low-level
radioactive waste to this proposed
site (which lies 20 miles from Mexican soil),
in exchange for which those two states would pay out
$25,000,000 (each) to Texas.

An old-timer in Ray's Bar told me how,
during the Great Depression of '33,
he'd 'rid the parallel truss-bars underneath
a boxcar of the Southern Pacific freight'.
I put another Lone Star on the tab
and he expatiated:

        Tham wus the days
whan one in five wus jobless an headin West.
Ya'd grip the iron truss-rods used to strenthen
the railroad cars – ya'd only be ten inches
off'n the rails. The trick wus gettin a board
an layin it across the horizontal
rods, so's ya'd hev a kinda shelf to lay on
face down, eyes closed against the flyin dirt
as blowed up off'n the track.

               A frenna mine

nodded asleep, rolled off, an skrithered along
under the wheels like butcher meat.

We flipped
the freights, we ditched the bulls, we decked the rattlers
an rid the rods. Thay called us bums an bos
an yeggs, an now it seems a long ways back...
Whan ya git old ya can't remember shit.

Encrypted – *thars a word the CIA*
uses tew mean thar sendin me in code
the latest information from the White House.
Thay sends it different ways. The Burro Lady
(ya know, the lady travels all around
by mule, folk say she carries all her things
on that thar burro, everythin she owns,
she even goes as far as Marathon
sleepin along the highway, all her stuff
just danglin off the burro, pots an pans
an raggy clothes an stuff, strapped on the mule,
ya see her sleepin trussed up like a bundle
smack by the highway), well, she oftentimes
signals tew me as she goes ridin by –   .
thay comes from Washington, tham signals, coded,
but mah ole Chevy here [he pats the dashboard]
decodes tham ole encrypteds, every one.

The indigenous salutation, *How y'all?*,
induces, when the first *frisson* of the drawl
wears off, a desire to puke against a wall,
or evacuate one's chitterling, or spawl.

Hawthorne in Marfa Public Library:

I sailed on the 'Niagara' out of Boston,
saluted by the guns on Castle Island,
to Liverpool in '53. But now
I miss my hillside and my pen. The British,
sodden in strong beer, have a conversation
like a plum pudding – stodgy, bilious.

El Paisano Hotel, corner of Highland,
completed 1930, designed by Trost
& Trost, El Paso, in grand quasi-Spanish
Baroque style, built around a central courtyard
with fountain, ornate, long ago fucked up.

In '55 they made the movie *Giant*
in these parts and the crew and cast put up
at El Paisano – in the now musty lobby
autographed fading snaps of quondam stars
(Rock Hudson, Jimmy Dean, Elizabeth Taylor...)
embellish the dirty yellow walls, alongside
the scruffy mop-heads of a Texas Longhorn
and a Bison (Bisons were extirpated here,

along with Indians, by about 1880).

The cobwebbed photo of a prize Hereford bull,
immortalised in 1950, when
he won the American Royal Show in Kansas,
testifies to his having been called Jug,
bred up by ol' man Mitchell's sons from Marfa.

[An old-timer in Ray's Bar told me how:]
Bout three, four years ago we wus called out
to just this side of Van Horn here on 90 –
Union Pacific'd gotten itself derailed.
State Troopers wus all thar as well as us
Fire Service critters, plus a buncha boys
out'n the Sheriff's Office.

                  Wayl, that wreck
really wus somethin – nobody wus hurt
but one tham freight trucks had been fulla brandy
an busted open. We fetched a fire truck full
back into town, an Sheriff an the Troopers
didn't go short I guess. I still got three
full gallon bottles a-waitin thar back home.

In '36 the Hotel building housed:
Bledsoe & Swearingem [I swear it!], Lawyers;
and W.B. Mitchell & Sons, Ranchers...
Hal Trost's anachronistic Baroque folly,
built for an oil boom that did not transpire.

Zane Grey, the author of Westerns, came to Marfa
a couple of times, researching for his book
The Lone Star Ranger, which he dedicated
to Jeff Vaughan – Ranger, Deputy U.S. Marshal,
Customs Official, Sheriff of Presidio,
served as a judge in the World Series Rodeo
at Madison Square Garden, N.Y. City.
Vaughan had a horse called Jack o' Diamonds, raised
on the Bite Ranch and famous for his style
and custom-crafted saddle with hand carvings
and fancy silver ornamental tooling.

Some feller I met in Ray's Bar told me how
one night, after a dozen or so Lone Stars,
as he was going for home, he saw Jeff Vaughan
on Jack o' Diamonds and Zane Grey on a *burro*
heading down Highland from the County Courthouse.
He mumbled 'How y'all?' and they said 'Howdy',
then rode, transparent, plumb through the Library wall.

Three locos, hundred-seventeen freight-cars,
discordant mile-long Union Pacific howl.

Editor:
I notice that Mr. Jeff Hubbard, in one of his Honest, Competent and Qualified advertisements for himself (Big Bend Sentinel, 10.15.98), perpetuates the solecism "miniscule" where minuscule is the mot juste.
Peter Reading
Marfa

Peter Reading

CUNT TWIRLY

The Big Bend Sentinel, Marfa, Texas, October 22, 1998

Jeff Hubbard for County Judge

Presidio County

Honest, Competent and Qualified

...my objective is to ...way to rape the ...le ...

protect private property ...
landowners of this dre... ...
ather than to...

vote for Jeff Hub...ward for
County Judge.

CUNT TWIRLY

To the Editor, the *Big Bend Sentinel* –
Late Saturday night some hoodlum element
daubed orange paint graffiti on several signs
which picture the prospective Candidate
for County Judge in the forthcoming poll,
Mr Jeff Hubbard. ['Twirly', our sobriquet,
occasioned by his brash mustachio.]
Scrawling such things is bad enough itself,
but when you realise that some of these
words by the 'midnight artists' are the most
dirty, obscene and blasphemous on earth,
it is intolerable! One of the signs
happens to be on 90 next to El Cheapo,
directly opposite the Catholic Church.
[Some wag had sprayed CUNT TWIRLY on the placard.]
Can you imagine what parishioners thought
when they drove in for Mass on Sunday morning?

Tham Marfa Lahbry folks tole may Zahn Grah
dahd Altadena, Californahyay,
bout nahnteen tharty nahn – s hah come that dude
in Ray's rickns hay seenm jis lays nah
on Hahlan rahdn a motherfucker *burro*?

The fins no longer spinning on the mast
of the Aermotor Windmill Company pump;
the circular, concrete-lined, brick water-tank
empty, dead *Corvus corax* in its dregs;

the ranch-house harbouring dead Horned Lizards, parched;
the shelf where a deceased Dude Rancher's Mescal,
half full, supports its fat worm in the lees...

You and I swig it, Johnston, and growl 'Cheers'
to the Old Boy who went stiff four years back.

A lone vexed longhorn bull, malevolent,
rattles the rotting, tied-together rails
round the corral, built about 1920
by the Galveston, Harrisburg & San Anton'
Rail Company. These defunct stockpens served
a central shipping point for animals raised
in Brewster, Presidio and Jeff Davis Counties.

As many as 70,000 head of cattle
were shipped from these yards in a single year.

Pens were enlarged in 1929
to handle the extraordinary expansion
of business.

By the '30s sheep and goats
were also being lugged from here. The trade
declined some after trucking was introduced.

The Stockyards are still used to weigh beasts prior
to shipment:

RAILROAD PENS, OWNED/OPERATED
BY FOWLKES'S CATTLE Co. (INCORPORATED)
RECEIVING STOCK 8 t' 3 WEDNSDAYS

OR BY REQQS r. rER ALL Yr TRUCKIN nEEDS.

A remedy for all that is not good:
Mezcal (also to celebrate good things).

(**Hubbard's opponent romps to victory** –
headline in this week's *Big Bend Sentinel*.)

Poor Twirly, pompous, puffed, opinionated,
yet, as the poll discloses clearly, hated.

On Highway 385 out of Fort Stockton,
going through Marathon to Persimmon Gap,
you are following the Great Comanche War Trail.

The savages drifted south into the Big Bend
during the 1840s–1880s
to raid *our* ranches, settlements, wagon trains,
both sides the Rio Grande.

                              Five miles south
of Marathon, Fort Pena Colorado
was built in '79 to nail the redskins.

The Southern Pacific Railroad Company
got here in '81, supplying the Fort
and ranches with essential guns and stores.

Since the Comanche has been extirpated
things hereabouts have been just hunky-dory –
the Chisos Gallery vends Ranch Antiques,
and Nicely Restored Cottages are for rent.

Wayl, ah woke up thays mornin kinda ahly,
sun wus jus rahzn over the water tower
makin it look pinksilver, kinda purdy.

Wayl, ah wus spose bay warkn foh ol Fowlkes
over the Cattle Pens, s ah tuke the Chev
an gt thar bout, oh, aytah clock ah gays.

Wayl, Longhorn bull in thah, bayn thah ahl nah,
purdy dam mean, hay hollered at may ten times –

wayl, the tenth letter of th alphybayt
is J, an, since mah naym is Jeremiah,
ah figure as hays atryin tew contac may
concernin sumptn from the CIA.

The crumbling tomb of Señora Prieto
piously venerated with a posy
of plastic roses in a Bud Light empty.

131

On 90 East from Marfa through to Alpine
a section of dense brush, low oaks and thorns
harbours Wild Turkeys. A covey of 15
females flaps heavily against driving rain
over the Chev, just clearing it by inches.
When I get home I'll fax this to you, Johnston,
then drain a 6 of Michelob in their honour.

Morning. Above this arid scrubland basin,
three dozen Sandhill Cranes, at about a thousand
feet, circle, bugle-croaking, south. Late Fall.

Presidio County Courthouse: on the Green,
a disgorged pellet of *Sylvilagus* bones;
above, in a long-established Cottonwood,
the privilege of a Great Horned Owl at roost.

[The quarterly *Desert Candle* carries this
story of a **West Texas Visitation**:]

Week before Christmas, 1996.
Juanita in her kitchen at Fort Stockton,
making tortillas for her family's dinner,
her mind not on the meal but on her son
(died in the line of Border Patrol duty
some years before) and of how terribly lonely
Christmas would be without him.

                              When she sat
at table with her family ready to eat,
she served a few tortillas and then noticed
one in particular – 'When I went to eat it,
I saw the donkey! I saw the ears and head,
and then the legs, and then I saw the Virgin
Mary riding, holding the Baby Jesus!'

It seemed to her that even in West Texas
Jesus comes visiting sometimes, that in this
Blessèd Tortilla was writ the Word of God.
So she has kept this epiphanous tortilla,
which lightened the burthen of her grief somewhat,
and has it still.

                    When, recently, in Alpine,
the *Desert Candle* made a photocopy
of the tortilla, the contrast in the print
clarified the image enough to see –
well, look for yourselves, examine the tortilla:
the *burro*, Mary, Jesus AND JOSEPH TOO!

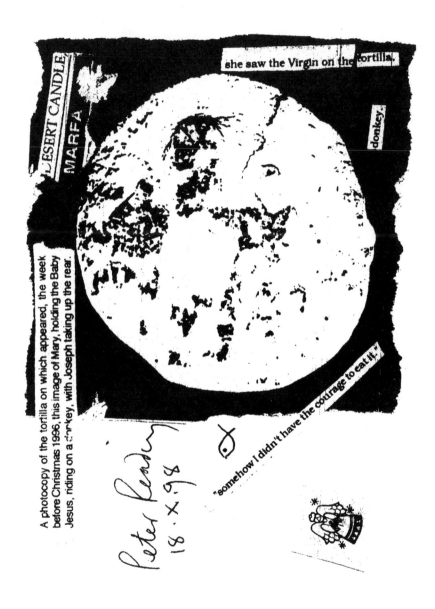

she saw the Virgin on the tortilla.

DESERT CANDLE, MARFA

donkey.

A photocopy of the tortilla on which appeared, the week before Christmas 1996, this image of Mary, holding the Baby Jesus, riding on a donkey, with Joseph taking up the rear.

"somehow I didn't have the courage to eat it."

Peter Reading
18 . X . 98

134

Every few hundred yards they dug a culvert
beneath the Southern Pacific line (in case
floodwater rose and flashed the track away),
and under one of these (just three feet high,
two beams with sleepers across them, rails exposed)
I lay down as four Union locos, linked,
howled a two-miler, hundred-twenty trucks,
like an infuriated Mastodon
above my head – the usual P & O,
Evergreen, N.O.L., Conco and Hanjin
containers, double-stacked, clattering over...

Scared myself shitless down there; quite amusing.

[From the Chinese in Marfa Library:]

The confidence of being unobserved
induces the bored poet to pick his nose.

You too can own a bloody plastic Jesus –
$5 down the Ave Maria Gift Shop.

'Undocumented Aliens' thay call em,
tham Spiks the Border Patrol nabbed yeastarday.

When Cabeza de Vaca crossed Big Bend
in 1535 these mortar-holes
in the Cretaceous limestone riverbank shelves,
cylindrical deep metates used for grinding
grain or mesquite beans, were already ancient.

It is not known what tribe, or if they lived
under these smoke-blacked sheer precipitous cliffs,
but that each time they pestled seed or legumes
their negative memorials deepened some.

Past Boulder Meadow the trail begins to switchback
up the South Wall. Beneath the peak it passes
between a stand of Bigtooth Maples. You drop
into Boot Canyon, residual Arcady,
after the heady crest of Pinnacles,
eroded stacks, and Pinyon, Juniper, Oak,
sheer steeps down near 8,000 feet below.
From Emory you see clear to Davis Mountains,
Marfa and Alpine and a hundred miles
into the smog of hapless Mexico.

Kickoff, the Shorthorns' great Homecoming game;
the martial clangor and the menacing drum;
they look like extras out of *Ivanhoe* –
bright helmets, visors, armoured shoulders, greaves,
tensed ready for the Tourney and the Tilt
in the grim Lists at Ashby-de-la-Zouch.

In Hicksville, real estate is snapped up – arties,
architects, carpet-baggers, entrepreneurs,
'gallery owners', leather coat boutiquesters...

The indigenous can fuck off outa here.

Lit by a horizontal sunrise shaft,
a Golden Eagle gleams from the highest perch
of that tall conifer across the street,
corner of Washington and North Plateau.
About this there is no more to be written.

Ah have mah copy of this month's *Christian Ranchman*
right heah, Cowboys foh Chras, ah thank y'all!,
an, bah the grace of God, ah know ahm saved!

Ah like thas cowboy styla preachin – how
ya finish ya devotions foh the day
with a bo-dacious buck off. But the hahlight
is knowin ya do God's work bah leadin folks
tew Jesus. Jesus heals tham who is hooked
on drink an rescues many, many souls!

Ah see an ad. heah foh a Guardian Angel
in gold or silver, wearin a stetson, jus
4 bucks – wayl ahl bay hog-tied; sen may wone!

Ah see wone heah foh Cowboys foh Chras belt-buckles
in antique bronze or silver with gold inlay,
sayn 'COWBOYS FOH CHRAS' an 'JESUS CHRAS IS LOWD'
writ thah right own the thayng – 35 bucks.

Ah see a testimowny framma sinna
whew foun God's Glory – it's a Glory Story!

An nah ah wans tew say a leel ol prar:

*Ah bin a cowpoke, Lowd, a long tahm, it seems,
aworkin an adreamin cowpoke dreams.*

*But lately, thars ahankerin in mah soul
foh tew git mahself rah unner Yoh control!*

*So, with mah spurs an chaps an hat in haynd,
ahm headin, with ol Blu, foh the Promiss Laynd.*

*Now thars a light in Hayvn ahm longn tew see
an ah heah Jesus calln – yep, foh me!*

Some loophole in the system here allows
the region's oldest industries to dodge
state air pollution legal regulations –
older facilities are not obliged,
if they were built prior to '71,
to meet the Texas Clean Air Act requirements
that 'best available control technologies'
be used. They were excluded, or 'Grandfathered',
from any newer, more exacting laws.
Grandfathered industries around the region
emit the same nitrogen oxide levels
as about 3 million motor cars, while coal-powered
Mexican Carbon I & II plants belch
more than 250,000 tons
of sulphur dioxide yearly into the mild
south-easterly breeze, which wafts it sweetly over
the Big Bend National Park and fucks it good.

Th BP boys is doin wayl agin –
th Marfa Sector pulled in three more on em,
Undocumented Spiks lookin fer wk.

[Headline in this week's *Big Bend Sentinel*:
Marfa hosts international architects.]

'The concrete used in the Marfa sewer plant
is just the same as Judd used in his pieces.
That shows that it is not the thing you use
but what you do with it,' explains Alexacos.

'This town is how it look because the buildings,'
Hazin Anuar is hasty to opine.

'I walk into a garage and I talk
happily to the owner,' says Onishi.
'If I do that in London, he have say
"Why, please, will you not quickly go away!"'

A newly dug up ancient Indian campfire,
this side of Alpine, was discovered when
the city sewer line was being surveyed.
The basin-shaped, intact Native American
hearth was revealed, 3 feet diameter,
placed in a shallow excavated pit,
constructed with vesicular laval basalt
and other cobbles. Charcoal fragments from it
were radiocarbon dated to the time
(during the Late Archaic, over here)
when the Nazarene was hammered to his tree.

[Someone I met in Ray's Bar cornered me:]

Ya know that Ol Cage next th Calaboose,
criss-cross black steel an kinda cubic-like,
7 by 7 foot by 7 foot,
with fold-dahn bunk-bayds one above th other
2 on each side (Sheriff ud lock ya in
t sober up, years back)? Wahl, me an Lopez
(ya know, the feller as busted Sharky's nose?),
wahd hayd a few too many Lone Stars, mebbie,
an moseyed that direction goin home,
an, bein overcowm with the fatigues,
layd dahn awhiles t sooth tham fevered brows
right thar on tham ol i-ron foldin bayds.

Slep thar all night an, risin aroun noon,
moseyed dahn t El Cheapo liquor store –
git us a 6 of Lones t take the cure.

It's Big-Time Art and small-town politics.

It's the *Highest Golf-Course in the Lone Star State*
(kept verdant by the lowest water table).

To the Editor, the *Desert Candle* – Sir,
your article concerning the tortilla
with revelatory powers was no big deal.
I have at home: a partially cooked chupatti
showing a living likeness of the Buddha;
great Krishna limned in a popadam; a nacho
clearly depicting Jupiter enthroned;
Mahomet's profile on a Hershey Bar;
and all Olympus in a blueberry muffin.

Look east, a five-Martini-sunset warms
our backs. Beyond our selves, beyond our booze,
beyond Roy Godbold's silvered and fiery silos,
beyond the arid basin, Cathedral Mountain
rears up to nearly seven thousand feet,
an intrusive mass of tilted Permian limestone,
200,000,000-year-old igneous rock,
crystalline, transient in this final lume.

Home base for viewing Marfa Mystery Lights!,
Thunderbird Motel, Restaurant, Trading Post,
Swimming Pool and access to the Highest
Golf Course in the whole of Texas (9 holes),
Cool Summers, Moderate Winters – see y'all!

Advisable to bring roach killer along;
the restaurant is shut; the pool drained empty.

142

The Courthouse is flammiferous for Christmas –
$25 will procure a flicker
to honour one whom you love and who is dead.

At Panther junction there's a massive tibia
of a Pterosaur which weighed 70 kilos
and had a 36-foot wingspan (more
than a small jet fighter).

                    In the late Cretaceous,
its shadow darkly traversed the Big Bend floodplain.

Look east, the sun, declining, warms our backs,
blushing the water tower's full, rounded bulk
flesh-pink, rose madder, lilac, Indian red –
like a woman's belly in a Bonnard bath.

The usually neglected Mexican tombs
have been attended-to this Day of the Dead:
each dry dirt plot and the little paths between,
fresh-raked like corduroy; bright new plastic blooms
replace the faded grey ones from last year;
a cross made from two sticks of Yucca is decked
with a pink ribbon; two days past Hallow-e'en,
some *hijo*'s pumpkin has become the head
of a hessian-bean-sack-robed unlikely saint
beside the concrete crucifix of a wrecked
vieja's grave, a sad, symbolic tear
bedewing the gourd's cheek in blue gloss paint.

[untitled]
(2001)

(Our runes, like theirs, will be uncipherable;
impartial Time will wipe the slate clean, wordless.)

Repetitious

Laertides bound daily to commute
with rolled umbrella, briefcase, pinstripe suit,
joining the train of apoplectic men.

And we have mixed among them on the quay,
placed pennies, at the turnstile, on our tongues,
walked clockwise, always clockwise, round the deck
until the plank is lowered and we file
into that city on the other side,
of smoke, tormented dummies and debris.

A woman called Kassandra met the plane,
welcomed them, warned them of the Ozone Hole
centred above Tasmania and showed
raw melanomas on her neck as proof –
none of them cared a nickel or a groat –
and they were told about the Thylacine
and the cute Forty-Spotted Pardalote...

(The only permanence is, I suppose,
in having been – and whether known or not
to others hardly enters into it.)

They dragged their craft's dark belly from safe shale
down to the fathomless expanse of brine,
locked into place the mainmast, set white sail,
loaded aboard a white tup, a black ewe,
then, at their nimble-witted captain's word,
embarked, leaden of heart and lachrymose.

Astern them rose a spanker-swelling breeze
surging the blue prow gulfward at 12 knots,
dependent on the helmsman and the drift
towards a smoke-enshrouded sunless port.

The bozo on the turnstile had black palms
from constantly receiving oboli.
They waded shoreward, reached Suburbia –
crushed polystyrene take-out trays, grease-smirched
fries-papers, Diet Pepsi cans, Man Pigs.

Here, daily, postmen scrunch the gravel path,
on the grimed lino wizened laurels scrape,
scripts are returned with vile rejection slips,
and seasons waste incontrovertibly.

They came to Mostar out of mountain sleet
into fecundity, peaches, vines, figs,
lamb carcasses spiked on slow-turning spits,
carp poached in spiced *bijelo vino* sauce.

A snow-haired elder strung his instrument,
the burthen of his song: malicious Fate
fucks up the aspirations of Mankind.

In Trebinje, all night, a Nightingale
solaced the Wily-Witted where he lay
drenched to the chine in vitriolic rain.

Dubrovnik harbour, where they moored the barque,
the Adriatic, violet in its depths,
wine-dark as *crno vino* which they sloshed
to toast Poseidon's generosity.

And in a quayside bar Jasmina's voice
whispered to him in Jug translationese
the burthen of some local blind man's song:

Surely the sly, resourceful mariner
peregrinated these blithe-scented isles,
inhaling fumous cypress, juniper,
tasting rich-clustered vines, salaciously
caressed by temptress most voluptuous,
and viewed with tears this ocean's endlessness
so very, very, very far from home.

Groped up the beach, brine-thrashed, until a bush
through which slashed sleet nor parching sun could pierce,
olive and oleaster grafted flush,
provided shelter. Crawled under dead leaves.
Exhaustion and oblivion combined –
thus does divine Athene comprehend
the frail necessities of Humankind.

This seems perpetual – the clashing rocks,
the maelstrom, then the landfall and the lust.

The one-eyed landlord will not let us out.
This sharpened picket should procure the deal.

(I grasp Achilles' hand, then realise
I am asleep and he is merely dead.)

This fucking thrumming Walkman in my brain! –
beeswax my ears and rope me to the mast!

So!, you would turn my mariners to pigs? –
just wait until I get you in that cave!

To Marfa, Texas, where they suffered much
deep in the desert, whose indigenous
subhumans garble inexactitudes
and do their petty business day by day
until the plank is lowered and they file
into that city on the other side.

After the butchery the suitors sprawled –
crans of blood-weltered washed-up drowning smelt
gulping for oxygen. By noon they stilled.

He told Telemachus to fetch the slags
and make them scrub the fancy furniture
clean of all shite and gore, then slay the cunts.

The nimble-witted and resourceful lad
rigged up a hawser from some dark-prowed barque
across the courtyard at about six feet

and there he dangled them on nooses – oh,
they twitched their little feet, but not for long.
The Master kissed Penelope and sang.

Petroglyphs,

long incomprehensible,
transient legacies pecked in the rockface.
Our Guide confirms their anonymity –
radiocarbon-dating lichen scars
suggests 5,000 years...

Last Wednesday,
a big pink dick was daubed on the same outcrop.

[untitled]

Proud warriors once   walked under these walls,
gone now for good,   their gear, their gods.
Their legions were brave,   they built bright palaces,
their days were soon done   and death undid them.
All on our earth   age and end,
even kings and kaisers   can't escape,
even a wizard   must go with his *Weird*.
Though a man bereft   may bury his brother
with gold garnered   throughout a good life,
the mouldering corpse   couldn't care less…
Proud warriors once   walked under these walls,
gone now for good,   their gear, their gods.

Alert!

With each dawn
the Klaxon howls
through gaps in the window-frame
and the inch under the door,
and the peace is shattered
and, dishevelled and starving,
with insomniac's eyeballs,
I plunge down the stairs four at once
and burst out gulping for breath with terror
into the street and run for dear life.

Each passing minute is my first and last –
it cannot be preserved
and I must be quick
for every step I take
may be my final one.

I must stay alive or Death will snatch me,
I must grab the last human
and wrench some utterance from his mouth.
But it is too late –
the duns are pounding my door
and I must run
or I'll be grabbed
by a bunch of street bums
begging me, not for cash or food
but for company in their bleak loneliness.

I run, shit scared,
chased by every quack in town –
they're after my blood for their patients.
I have to rush
to join the human flesh
brought daily in lorryloads
like fruit to the market.
I must run –
they're rounding up all the hobos and bums.
Someone has stolen my passport –
I can't get to the Passport Office
before it shuts.

I've lost my wristwatch,
nobody is here to ask what time it is;
each night they change the street names;
what shit has locked the park gates?;
I'm dizzy in the mornings,
there are no doctors;
my eyes, though, are powerful,
so powerful they hurt;
but my ticker is dodgy,
my teeth decaying,
my cough gets worse daily,
I'm getting thin on top,
I've got the shakes,
I look like an old fart...

But I run through the streets
of a world I can't live in,
a world at once seductive and alien,
where worldly things are miracles and coincidences,
where, in costly stores,
a myriad of mysterious
electronic gadgetry
lies in wait under its protective glass
to trap us.
Nothing is as it seems;
nothing fits me;
shoes are too small,
clothes too big;
I am a risible fool
following a coffin,
scared to look in the mirror,
nobody here to heed my ravings.

But I still run
along this endless street,
where a middle-aged no-hoper like me
sits solo like God in front of the shut church
and genuflects.
I grow tired,
get breathless,
wind slashes me,
It is cold, lonely.

I lose my way in this city,
though there's nowhere to go anyway,
and there's nobody to ask the way
because I don't know where the hell I'm going
and nobody understands my accent
nor I theirs.

But I continue running,
pass two men on a bridge,
pause, ready to share my happiness with them,
get stabbed in the shoulder for my trouble
and say Good Morning again.

Nobody phones me,
nobody requires my prowess –
I'm a roadbuilder,
drive JCBs through swamps, mountains,
though I call myself 'self-employed'
I don't work for *me*.
At weekends I write letters
(which nobody ever answers).
I sleep in short fits
punctuated with nightmares
(but I never take pills).
I own no books
(but once had an encyclopaedia),
I have one bed, one table,
one chair, one phone.
Cluttering the place are matchboxes
(full, empty),
bits of old sandwich,
coffee cups.
I don't smoke or drink or have a TV set.
Three candles last me all year.
All day I whistle cheerfully.
I can't put two words in order
to make sense.

All the time my phone rings
but never for me –

always the wrong number,
'Hello, yes, yes,
I'm the number you dialled.'
'No.'
I'm ex-directory.

So I sit with my candle by the window
and stare at the empty night
(it is a huge wiped blackboard).
Winter is icy; summer sweltering.
I suppose I seem like
some kind of dangerous nutter
to the whores who pick me up,
take me to their rooms,
clean me up then giggle
at my pathetic cock –
'Turn the light off!', I bellow
(they obey out of pity
or out of fright)
and I try to fuck in the dark,
but worry and fear
have rendered me impotent.

I am running, running still...
a legacy of sadness, tragedy,
anger and imagination
inherited from my parents –
my Old Chap said:
'He smells of Death;
that looks like blood on his hands;
mark my words, he'll revolt against his father,
he'll end up some kind of fucking artist!'

And the Klaxon is howling,
and I continue running, running...
I have to get to work or I'm sacked.
They're making a new road
and I rush on, fucking and blinding.
I feel unwanted, unhappy,
on the way out.

I'm no use, a waste of time;
when I go to bed I lock the door twice,
look in every nook and cranny, just in case;
if I hear a sound I'm terrified,
an insomniac without appetite.

But *inside*,
love and vigour quicken me,
stop me from thinking –
I'm not a clever man (just a B.A.),
uncultured, frequently sound like a twerp,
don't crack gags or enter into debates,
don't daydream or frivolously indulge,
don't stockpile knowledge,
but follow my *imagination*
far from all these shitters
to achieve something bigger.
So I retreat into my memory –
legends of sunk castles, ships' treasures,
treks to unknown regions
of sound, colour and words.
All these combat my grief and grossness,
enable me to join my fellow humans.
I feel like a leper, guilty.
In the street, at the movies, I'm jostled by a bunch of shits
(not that I care a toss,
I'm just different,
old fart but clean,
shoes worn out from running, but shined,
two shirts, one suit, one tie,
an individual life
that nobody knows anything about).

So I run, free and easy,
looking for – I don't know what
until I find it –
something that has had me searching
through Philadelphia's streets
collecting all the lunacy
from newspapers in trash cans
and from all the drunk down-and-outs in doorways,

searching beyond the horizon
for the last messenger who hasn't had
his tongue cut off, his eyes gouged out.

Dispatch Rider!
Courier of the vital (maybe final) message!
Budge up on your saddle and let's be off,
head for my apartment, we'll write the letters,
then back to the streets
to see the ten-o-clock starters emerge –
the powerful, pinstriped young fellers,
the little gods of lucre and manipulation
who will tread you underfoot,
march in ranks over your torn up lives.

And still I run.
My garret has no doorbell, nobody visits,
investigative agents are hounding me
but of course they don't know where or how to nab me.
The ones they *do* invariably manage to nick
are the small-time arsonists, the muggers, the dips,
the pathetic indecent assaulters, the homicides...
They bundle them into stir until it bulges.
But I'm the one they *should* be worried about,
the one who knows what the Klaxon means and awakes
and pursues the enemy down labyrinthine alleys,
the enemy who gambles our lot in 'Vegas,
who fritters the profits and lives of the people who pay
and pay and pay and pay for it till they die,
the people forced to live in crammed conurbations
so as to be, perhaps, less vulnerable
than if they had to face it alone and naked.

I scrawl this in my letters to all and sundry:
    Don't quake in fright at those who may *look* as imposing
    and awe-inspiring as knights in protective armour,
    who try to tangle you up
    in a net of regulations, laws and bullshit –
    in *fact* there's no more to them
    than a bunch of feeble mousefarts.

Whatever you see is only the mirage
of the thing behind it.
You want to phone, but don't have a dime;
you've shouted Bingo!, but lost your card;
you want to stay, but the motel's full;
you quit the cinema, the movie's still rolling;
don't pray if you don't know *who* you're praying to;
laugh or cry – nothing in between –
every grin is a compromise;
above all be patient, await my arrival.

One of these mornings,
when the *real* alarm sounds,
I shall pack, lock up, set out and not return.
As usual, I shall run,
but this time not like some frantic jogger,
not like some fleeing felon,
not like some nut-case
such as the mad spinning of the city
hurls right out of the social system.
This time I'll tread
with the precision of a tight-rope walker,
I shall shake you awake,
I'll hold you upside down by the feet
and slap your arse
until I know you're properly re-born,
I shall pinch you until, startled into noticing,
you grow aware of, appreciative of,
all that the world offers,
I'll prise your eyelids open
so you can't continue sleeping.

All of you, assemble at the hall
(like the blacks gather each evening on 52nd),
await my arrival, whenever that may be.
Together we'll round up:
all the shyster lawyers;

all the indulged phoney artists;
all the hypocrite sky-pilots;
all the academics who spout shite;
all the slipshod tabloid journalists;
all the eighth-rate assholes who've contributed
to this universal fucking con trick –
we'll round, round them up and exile them to hell for keeps!

By doing this
we shall seize truth, after its long absence,
be able, at last, properly to see,
touch, smell, love.
You have patiently awaited my arrival;
and although, inevitably,
I must quit eventually (who knows when?),
someone will replace me.
This cause is a matter of life and death,
I deeply sympathise, my friends,
I know you've had to wait so long
for a miracle like this to happen –
the engendering of this spirit,
where frustration, anger and impatience
can no longer be contained!

What's this?
The curtain won't rise – faulty mechanism?,
some sort of dispute?, anyway the hall's empty.
Is it too late?, too early?,
is someone taking the piss?
No matter – let's make the best we can of it.
Trust me, I'll act with you and prompt at the same time.
I must get even with man and god –
not that I'm bitter or revengeful,
merely feel depressed, downtrodden,
while, despite fine speeches and sentiments,
nothing happens and we grow tired and grey.

Listen! I'm not a fat rich man,
I don't *look* much but I'm sincere –
we have only hunger to eat
and trash for dessert,
those who think they've 'found god' better throw in the towel,

what we see up front is merely mirage,
the sexy, the succulent, mirage, mirage.
Listen!, you dumbos,
you shuffle your feet, you check your watches, talk crap –
who do you think you're kidding?
What you're pursuing is shit.
All of a sudden, though, it dawns on you:
that new hotel is *still* unfinished,
it should have been opened months ago,
have they gone bust?, has the builder fucked off?,
nobody knows, nobody knows.
Life is the mirage behind which Death lurks;
when the mirage clears
there'll be only one ridiculously simple question
and nobody to ask it or answer.

I shall tell you of all these things
upon my arrival.
Although it embarrasses me, I shall tell you –
you see I'm as stubborn as a mule
(walking the precipice edge is nothing to me)
and I'll set off an alarm
that you will have to pay attention to.
Let's see if we can raise the curtain
just a little and glimpse at least
one scene, one speech, one word...
Already I am forty-odd,
will I ever grow up?,
will I ever stop panicking?, ever rest?,
stroll instead of run, run, run?
Who really cares two shits for a beached fish
thrashing on the shingle, gulping for oxygen?

You shall all witness and believe when I appear to you;
twenty-four hours a day the alarm clock will ring out,
nearly driving you mad;
your brain will be emptied by devouring rats;
you will learn to endure
tantalising agonies
in order to prepare you
for the rigours of my expedition.

I'm not macho,
but I can resist any onslaught;
I may bend, but never break;
I may look like a circus clown,
but I'm self-possessed.
In my nonage I frittered away my wealth,
my ideals and any vestige of religion –
a latter-day prodigal,
except that I didn't return to the fold,
went off to meditate up in the mountains,
came down to earth again to join in the world's shit.

Wait now and be ready;
the Klaxon will sound off one fateful dawning
and you'll run into the street –
you know the rest.

*

Well, I can say no more:
each utterance is fractured,
incomprehensible, unfinished –
like its utterer, maimed in its intent.
But, you know,
there's another level above mere utterance
to which only I have access and understanding.

The less of *me* the better:
The Times leaves wither on my desk;
my eyes see so much they hurt;
is it dusk, or dawn?;
I await the Klaxon.

(from Vahé Oshagan's literal English rendering of his own Armenian poem.)

Hispanic

When the gipsy Preciosa
thrums her tambourine
honeyed sound sweetens the formerly empty air –
pearls from her fingers,
sweet blooms from her lips issue.

*

Amiga, the saplings,
the sapling osier bed.
Under the sapling osiers, *amiga*,
two close friends have passed...

and have gone now together
to verdant meadows
out from the sapling osier bed,
amantes.

*

In May, May, time of the heatwave,
when lovers lay openly out in the meadowlands,
I lay deep in a dungeon, not knowing
day from darkness – except for a little bird
who melodied me each chill dawn.

An archer pierced her heart. God give him shit!

[untitled]

Styx, Acheron, Cocytus, Phlegethon
and Lethe – these we crossed by divers ferries
('Charon & Co., prompt service guaranteed').

Entirely silent, unaccompanied,
my guide and I walked one behind the other,
like Friars Minor in some lightless cloister.

We made our way along a jagged crag,
narrow, precipitous and difficult,
more hideous than anything before.

Now I talked loudly, not to appear afraid,
when a coarse growl issued out of the deep moat,
garbling, inarticulate and hoarse –

what was the burthen of it I don't know,
but bitter wrath was certainly apparent.
And now we crossed some perilous viaduct,

and though I peered down still I couldn't see
a limit to the vast depth of that gulph.
I to my guide: 'Must we go further down?'

And he to me: 'Yes.' Whereupon I saw
a mob of festering reptilians,
memory of which still chills my troubled sleep.

Among these violent and these dismal things,
people meandered naked and afraid
with hope of neither exit nor of light.

Out of the filthy slime a figure rose:
'Who are you that arrives before his hour?',
then slithered back into the fetid slough.

'Have we now viewed the full extent of Hell?'
My guide to me: 'You ain't seen nothing yet.'

Hispanic

In the awe-inspiring nave
of the Byzantine church
(tomb of a supine lady,
her flesh and her dress,
her soft skin, lace and velvet,
cunningly rendered in marble)
I considered eternal death.

Copla a Pie Quebrado,

metric, the final foot broken –
fitting for history fractured
    in an aridified dump.

During the Permian, shallow
ocean flushed over this basin
richly depositing corpses –
    trilobites, brachiopods...

Out of dry fossils sprout yucca,
Texan *H. sap.*, ocotillo,
scorpions, chiggers, pursuing
    old depositional trends.

During the Upper Cretaceous,
continent bucklings round here
heralded ocean withdrawal
    causing dense vegetal growth –

marshes, ferns, mosses, canes, forests.
Crocs, *Phobosuchus*, prowled Big Bend.
65 million years later,
    Eddie Pierce Motors vends Chevs.

Multiple layers of crazed paint
stain the old Mohair Shed facia:
palimpsest manuscript; scrivened
    prophecy in a lost code;

pictograph/petroglyph; runic
utterance sandblasted wordless;
sacrosanct hieroglyph rubric
    faded to meaningless slur.

Back of the Chevrolet dealer's:
arid cherts, anhydrous grasses,
busted up windshields and fenders,
    carcasses, silicate shards.

[Scholars unearthing the City
dug up the Dairy Queen milk bar,
chanced upon numerous treasured
    archaeological finds:]

Blueberry Caramel Fudgies,
Raspberry Snottyo Cookies,
Nuttyplop Whip Butterwhangers,
    Bumpy Bananadip Slimes,

Busterbar Dillybowl Sundaes,
M&Ms Spunkywhip Snickers,
Peanutty Chockydick Willies,
    Cherryspawl Caramel Squits.

old depositional tendence;
arid cherts, anhydrous grasses;
busted up windshields and chassis;
    carcasses, silicate shards

archaeological siftings;
History closed for the season;
metric, the final foot shattered,
    faded to meaningless slur

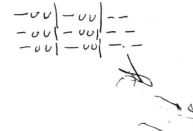

Small Change

Alcaic

Great Dionysus, master anaesthetist,
no more delay, fetch wine from the amphora,
    blend it with water in the krater,
        serve me a generous brimming skyphos.

[untitled]

Your *Weird* is beyond you;
what you *can* control
do prudently and consider the end.

From the Chinese

    His liver/
  his golden wine –
civil war rages!

Hibernian

Two conundrums:
a herring devoid of bones;
a life without the troubles.

LFC , Booby Jill SUCK!,Chazza,Fatz Kooly,
Wiite Shit.

rustle of old gratuitous scrivenings

Pink & fluorescent blue aerosol-written runic
sublingus:

Cadder shag the die; Krude de Wankers Death to
frail wisps of dead beatraked leaves all Kop Boots,

crackle of anhydrous bily

— · ·|— · ·|—
Croxley pa pyrus and bond

‖— ·· |— ·· |—

⟨רֶסַרַלֹ⟩·לֹפַּלֹ.ON·l∨·◁Ⅎ∕O↗

‖— ·|— ··|—

PERDUTA

Tatican
Inscription on a bowl: food uno pocato, cra careto (Latin Hodie
vinum bibam, cras carebo). "Today I shall drink wine, tomorrow
I shall have nothing."

[untitled]

Rough sacking, serving as a door, was lifted
revealing Gipsy Moses tracing ciphers
on crumbling sheets of vellum or papyrus,
forming crude runes like things dimly remembered...

Weird hieroglyphs pecked in the 'Roony Stane'
outside the Horseshoe, where some skilful mason
has managed to incorporate a tablet
of long-forgotten Saxon origin
into the mounting-block where all must see it...

Lost utterances – or not yet understood –
half to reveal/half to conceal the truth.

21. i. 2000 (0400–0500 hrs.)

A slowly consuming shadow falls across
the preternaturally rubicund
Near Side, obliterates the Bay of Rainbows,
the Lake of Dreams, smothers Serenity,
Tranquillity and Nectar, totally.

[untitled]

Shaving-mirror. Hmmm.
Known you since you were *this* high.
55?, so soon?
Seems like only yesterday
(of course it was all fields, *then*)...

Badass and not nice to know –
you have got used to the role.

[untitled]

In unmarked graves and splendid catafalques
alike, impartial atoms metamorphose.

Well, I can say no more:
each utterance is fractured,
incomprehensible, unfinished –
like its utterer, maimed in its intent.
But, you know,
there's another level above mere utterance
to which only I have access and understanding

The less of me the better:
The Times leaves wither on my desk;
my eyes see so much they hurt;
is it dusk, or dawn?;
I await ████ ████████.

Peter Reading

177

Graffiti

Les Grottes de Niaux are closed this Saturday.
A *carte postale illustrée*, though, depicts
wild horses, bison speared...

                                                Outside the cave,
kids carve a Zeppelin dick on the same rock –
Still, after 20,000 years, inclined
to score some mark on anonymity.

Dog's Tomb

```
┌─────────── ─────┐
│                  │
│     ι 'ic laʋet:  │
│                  │
│     Qu' ʋaeʋu    │
│  ʋt Senecti e     │
│    C ɯɪ.ʋcf s.   │
│                  │
└─────────── ───┘
```

Under a dripping Yew, a sandstone tablet
9 inches x 8 inches, the inscription
eroded, packed with moss, just legible:
QVI CAECVS ET SENECTVTE CONFECTVS.
Who blindness and senility prepared
for darkness and insensibility.

[untitled]

This very simple
axiom: *They live, then die;*
your love is powerless.

Homme de Lettres

back 22,000 years,
the Lascaux sophisticates;
next, Neolithic *calculi*
(stones incised for counting);
this tablet, about 2000
BC, charts the loan of donkeys;
pictographic trees,
sacks of grain, the god-man;
1450 BC,
the Elephantine Calendar;
525 BC,
cuneiform on silver;
'Chinese script conformed
with a series of subtle rules
which you could call *Poetic Art*';
the Greeks, the Romans, Gutenberg...

removed from semantic context,
the word = the visual

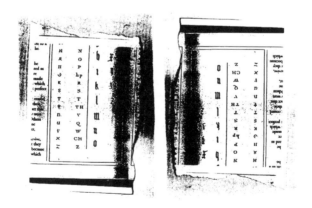

(today) I shall drink wine: tomorrow I shall have (none)

ΟΤΔΛΤΙ? · ΟΤΔ717 · ΟΝΙΛ · ΛΙΟΤ

(Faliscan)
inscription on drinking
bowl/cup

From Chinese

His liver/
has golden wine -
civil war rag...

alcaic

Great Dionysus, master anaesthetist,
no more delay, fetch wine from the amphora,
  blend it with water in the krater,
    serve me a generous brimming skyphos.

Apophthegmatic

Soon dry,
our shallow spring.

Bright spring day!
I contemplate fall.

Fall?, so soon?;
senile reflections;
geese fly south.

Autumn; plaintive cries
of migrant fowls; frightened eyes
of fish on the slab.

Old reaper,
bent like his own scythe;
late autumn.

Just for one
moment the scyther
hesitates...

Geese against dusk sky –
a will's words penned on parchment
sealed with wax full Moon.

Shaving-glass:
Time's snow creeps down cheeks.
Sharp razor.

Entering this world
the baby is washed, as is
the exiting corpse.

*

No Zen pretension
(though I squat in this wild place
on a thick moss mat,
drink wine and scorn ambition,
contemplate fall and brown leaves).

*

Why go
anymore to
        Deadwood?

    On my desk,
shrivelled laurel leaves.

                *

    Eschew luggage, for
the expedition is brief.

                *

Bosque del Apache:
10,000 Sandhill Cranes,
30,000 Snow Geese,
ripe Pinot Noir sunset –
why bother to scrawl verse?

                *

Drone of a chainsaw,
fumosity of pine sap –
    Mortimer Forest.

       *

Dark portentousness:

   on the cross above
the spire of Blessèd Specious
    a Great Horned Owl hoots,
defecates copiously;

   hydrogen sulphide
outodours the thurible –
    even prelates fart;

   bronze Buddha outside
a mountain shrine – from your nose
    hangs icicle snot.

       *

Obiit:

chiselled incisions packed
with lichen.

*

Hic Iacet:

*Qui Caecus
et Senectute
Confectus.*

*

Obiit:

mouldered to senselessness,
slick wordplay

*

Here lies...

By Blind Old Age
    Worn Out

          *

Obiit:

a palimpsest,
        shadow.

          *

Hic Jacet:

Who Blindness
of Soul by
    Exhausted.

          *

190

Obiit:

moulded to senselessness,
    slick wordpl…

*

Hic Iacet:

    Qui Caecus
et Senectute
    Confectus.

*

Obiit:

ci… …d i… …is… …s packe…
    …with hid…en.

*

Hic Jacet:

Who Blindness
& Senility
Exhausted.

*

Obiit:

a palimpsest,
or shadow.

*

Here lies…

By Blind Old Age
Worn Out.

*

Macedon **Philip**
(thrashed the Greek coalition
  at Chaeronea,
achieved an uneasy peace).

Philip (Apostle,
present when the 5,000
  guzzled buns and sprats).

Philip (dubbed Loudmouth,
husband of Elizabeth).

Philip (my brother,
in a Kent ward enduring
  chemotherapy,
restive, without appetite,
  glumly taciturn).

*

By the contrivance
of the telescope's wrong end
  Earth shrinks to a dime.

*

Your portrait of me,
Peter Edwards, is too good –
    makes me look like shit.

                *

cypher scrawl
        sered leaf
palimpsest
        ash scroll
tablet scratch –

    conceit
of **word-hoard**

                *

    Birthday card –
autumn still life
        with dead leaves.

                *

Even this slight Winter Wren
sipping the Rio Grande
alters the great river's flow.

*

I latch tight the door
of my microcosmic hut –
vernal with the spring,
in autumn feeling the fall.

*

Mortimer Forest: often
the chainsaw's drone, but, so far,
the sawyer unencountered...

today in the umbrageous
gloom of a lost path
I meet him head-on.

*

The payment is cleared;
after this 53rd year
all income is gain.

*

Soon I will not need
anymore to flick the flies
from my stupid self.

*

It is a lament –
hear the reeds under the moon

[He did not finish.]

*

196

Swaddle the newborn,
swaddle the wax cadaver

[He did not finish.]

*

Playing the word-games
in the watches of the night –
what a fucking lark!

*

Screwed-up parchment,
service to humankind –
discarded verse.

*

All those Nip stage-props!:
frogs, moons, herons, clear cascades
     (*kiyotaki ya*),
plum blossom, calligraphy...

You go, I stay – two autumns!

                    *

     Bittern stiff in reeds,
for ninety minutes we watch –
     in that time just three
cautious slow-motion high-steps,
three dagger stabs, three tadpoles.

                    *

     this
frail vessel
     drifts

                    *

Life is a loan,
as the *Seafarer* knew.
Duns pound the door.

*

ʰic lacet:

Quʰ Caerus
et Senectuʰe
C ʰirecʰ s.

*

Petroglyph –
pecked cyphers obscured
by lichen.

*

Hic Jacet:

Taciturnity
　　his virtue.

＊

　　The arbitrary
nature of syllabic verse –
　　and the brevity!

FAUNAL

(2002)

'We will now discuss in a little more detail the struggle for existence...'

CHARLES DARWIN,
The Origin of Species

On Bruny Island, off Tas.,

we were driving along a dirt road
to locate a breeding pair
of Forty-spotted Pardalote
when we damn near hit an Echidna
(Tachyglossus sestosus)
snuffling into the verge grass.

We got out to scrutinise it,
inhale its stink and consider
this marvellous monotreme
and all elegant biodiversity.

Neighbourhood Watch

'...let it profit thee to have heard,
By terrible example, the reward
Of disobedience; firm they might have stood,
Yet fell; remember, and fear to transgress.'
MILTON,
Paradise Lost

Those loafers, corner-boys, do-nothings, bums,
drones, idlers, layabouts, thugs, loungers, wastrels,
time-wasters, shirkers, ne'er-do-wells, yahoos,
yobs, yobbos, hallions, churls, hobbledehoys,
dossers, delinquents, swads, louts, hooligans,
unemployed tosspots, hoodlums, rowdies, scums,
have got away with too much for too long,
the neighbourhood is going to the dogs.

The PM wants to see the squeegee merchants
(who lurk at traffic lights to accost your windscreens)
eliminated. Beggars he finds repulsive,
offensive to the sensibility –
these 'homeless' people simply are a nuisance
and should be done away with so that decent
members of the community don't see them
and feel distressed.

He never gives to beggars,
but once purchased a copy of the *Big Issue*
which caused him a virtuous *frisson* for a week.
He knows it's right to be intolerant
of vagrants – it's appalling that young people
are to be found in grimy sleeping-bags
in decent people's doorways. He will clear
the streets of 'winos', 'alcos', 'dossers', 'addicts'.

– Is there a Third Way? We believe there is.
The welfare system, as we well perceive,
is wasteful and inappropriately addictive.
Social Security benefits encourage
a culture of dependency, you see.

Public expenditure (thus Blair and Schröder,
in 1999, express concern)
has reached the limits of the acceptable.

He'd fine graffiti artists on the spot –
how would you feel if your mother read such things?,
the neighbourhood would be a darned sight better
if thugs like this were fined or put away
and decent folk could stroll the unsullied streets.

The lager louts who kick your garden gate
and bellow down the road on Friday nights
and chuck the orange traffic cones about
and sometimes even take their trousers down
facetiously displaying insolent buttocks,
he thinks should be arrested by stout bobbies,
marched to the nearest cash point and required
to contritely withdraw £100
each and convey it to the officers.
[Which jackass proposition may well prove
more difficult to enforce than to dream up.]

The hallions are more than an aesthetic
displeasure, they represent the end of us;
the hallions are hammering at the door;
the neighbourhood is going to the dogs.
[But more than electoral bluster is required
to arrest the momentum of this gathering maelstrom.]

Field Note

I riffle my notebooks' leaves now at my desk:

A page erased, eroded, foxed, forgotten.

[Untitled]

They sprawl round the pool;
I seek arboreal shade –
   less melanomas.

                    *

Last night I dreamed of the red-finned, bronze-girthed Rudd
for which we fished in the Marl Pond when we were blithe.
But now, my brother, I think you are dying –
four-fifths of your stomach to the scalpel,
your back bent double with chemo.

                    *

The dark shore white with
Larus atricilla, you,
   child, throwing them bread.

Only the Laughing Gulls, now.

                    *

Japanese art buffs
emerge from the Van Gogh show
clutching prismatic cartons
   emblazoned **Vincent**
containing rolled up posters –
the rich harvest molested
   by malign corvids.

That find of *Longisquama insignis,*

oldest known feathered fossil evidence,
from a reptilian creature which most likely
glided between the trees in forest swamps
75 million years pre-*Archaeopterix*
in Central Asia, anticipated birds.

It had a furcula virtually the same
as modern birds, and *wasn't* a dinosaur.

What was the initial function of those feathers
(whose evolution probably antedates
the dinosaur)? Did they develop from scales
for insulation when warm blood arrived?
Or did these nascent plumes burgeon from ridges
along the back, and muscles then develop
in forelimbs, coincident with plumage growth,
enabling first flight?...

            Sunt aliquid manes.

Anthropological

We anchored in a bay under the island
and, on our way to shore, pulled alongside
a group of abject natives in a canoe.

These tribes possess no fragment of attire
and go quite naked. Rain was falling hard,
and this, together with the spray combined,
ran down their naked bodies in rivulets.

In another harbour, distant about a league,
a woman, suckling a new-born child,
came alongside the vessel and drifted there
while sleet fell and thawed on her nakedness
and on the tender skin of her bare baby.

These hapless wretches, stunted in their growth,
had hideous faces daubed with gaudy paint,
their skins engrimed with filth, their hair entangled,
their voices harsh, discordant, ululant,
their gestures violent, lacking dignity.
Watching such men, one scarcely can believe
that they are fellow-creatures inhabiting
the same world.

            It is commonly conjectured
what pleasure life affords to lower species:
how much more reasonably the very same
question may be applied to these barbarians.

At night some five or six of these poor beings,
naked and unprotected from the wind
and lashing rains of this tempestuous climate,
sleep on the wet ground, curled like trembling curs.

Whenever it is low water, they must rise
to harvest shellfish from the rocks; the women,
winter or summer, dive to collect sea eggs,
or, shivering, sit with baited lines to jerk
small fishes from the water into their boats.

Should the putrid carcass of some floating whale
be found, it is a feast, guzzled with relish,
accompanied by a few sour berries and fungi.
Famine is frequent, and, in consequence,
cannibalism and parricide prevail.

No government or head men are there here,
but hostile neighbours, speaking in different thoughts.

Their warfare is occasioned by the lack
of jealous-guarded pitiful resources.

Frontiers reflect past acts of butchery.

Their country is a broken mass of rock
viewed through the gloomy mist of endless storms.

In search of food they are compelled to roam.

To knock a limpet from a rock requires
no towering intellect.

                        Their base condition
is nowise bettered by experience.

They are at once vile and intractable.

Congress Avenue Bridge in Austin, Texas,

Mexican Free-tailed Bats,
Tadaria brasiliensis (mexicana),
over one million of them
at dusk emerging from roost-slots under the span.

They formed a granular trail
dispersing into the dark.
One of the most spectacular
phenomena I have ever been privileged to witness.

I threw the Zeiss in the Colorado River
(after 38 years they were ruined from sea-spray and grit –
I remember, one time, their slithering into a rock-pool
while I was busied banding a Purple Sandpiper)
and then became drunk to celebrate the occasion.

The Sheriff's Department dealt with the peccadillo
(six hours stuck in stir
with a bunch of Mexican kids on a charge of Possession).

When I got out it amounted to two hundred dollars
(Public Intoxication).

Along the river
early next morning (I had the Bausch & Lomb
to replace the Zeiss) a Sora was stalking the reeds.
Overhead, Scissor-tailed Flycatchers
foretold the fall migration.

Cetacean

Out of Fisherman's Wharf, San Francisco, Sunday, early,
our vessel, bow to stern, some sixty-three feet,
to observe Blue Whales – and we did, off the Farallones.

They were swimming slowly, and rose at a shallow angle
(they were grey as slate with white mottling, dorsals tiny and stubby,
with broad flat heads one quarter their overall body-lengths).

They blew as soon as their heads began to break the surface.
The blows were as straight and slim as upright columns
rising to thirty feet in vertical sprays.

Then their heads disappeared underwater, and the lengthy, rolling
expanse of their backs hove into our view – about twenty feet longer
than the vessel herself.

And then the diminutive dorsals
showed briefly, after the blows had dispersed and the heads had
gone under.

Then they arched their backs, then arched their tail stocks ready
for diving.

Then the flukes were visible just before the creatures vanished,
slipping into the deep again, at a shallow angle.

Thanksgiving

That day on the coast of Veracruz,
within a single hour,
into the bright crisp focus
of the Bausch & Lomb 8-42s:
a Magnificent Frigatebird
(adult male, glossy black,
red throat pouch, bifurcate tail)
above a hurricane-shunted
vast sand dune, and, below,
quartering open scrubland,
an Aplomado Falcon
(slate crown, white eyebrow and chest,
black flanks, cinnamon belly),
and, perched on a string of barbed wire,
a Fork-tailed Flycatcher
(black tail-plumes twice its body-length,
black cap, pure white underparts).

And for this I gave, and give, thanks
to *Fregata magnificens,*
to *Falco femoralis,*
to *Tyrannus savana*
and to William Johnston – *¡Amigo!*

Beethovenstraat,

outside the Fidelio Bar
sipping a gelid beer.

Suddenly overhead,
long tails, jet-fighter flight,
skree-ik, skree-ik, skree-ik –
Rose-ringed Parakeets
hurtle above the traffic
(Afro/Asian species,
Psittacula krameri,
feral here, they breed
freely in Vondelpark).

In acknowledgement of which
epiphanic event,
Een ander Amstel, alstublieft.

Lit.

You know that it's time to pack up
when the shelves in the shops are stocked
with titles like *Give Us A Break!*
by an osteopath named Berk,
and *Ashtrays Through The Ages*
by Vladimir Hogsnot-Smoke.

Educative

One day, when I was ten or thereabouts,
the Natural Science teacher, Mrs Hope,
assisted by the *Bug-Eye*, as we fondly
dubbed *Caliban* the Caretaker, turned up
trundling an ancient epidiascope
which she proceeded to plug in, adjust,
and focus until a rectangle of light
was dimly projected on the classroom wall.
Within the bright glow of the apparatus
she conjured a large illustrated book
until an image, furry, indistinct,
became apparent on the impromptu screen.

Children, these are serious times indeed...

It had been, once, a coney, but was now
a distorted, swollen, slimy face with eyes
bulging and blind (not *that* dissimilar
to those of the hapless Janitor).

                                     Years on,
the distemper reached an island off the coast
of North Wales where I helped to break the backs
and pitch the bodies of the unfortunate,
infected creatures over the East Face cliff...
(We are all members of the Wildlife Trust.)

Forty more years, a Trustee is defining
Myxomatosis: *Viral disease in rabbits;*
produces fever; lesions of the skin
resembling myxomas; muscoid swelling
of mucous membranes; it exists in nature
in South American species of the genus
Sylvilagus, *and has been introduced*
to parts of Europe and Australia
as a means of rabbit population control...

Ladies and Gentlemen, back in '54,
an article in The Times *of July 1st*
reports that: 'Myxomatosis, this past year,
has extirpated 90 per cent of burrows
in southern England alone. Farmers insist
that this is a virus vital in the control
of rabbits, which do vast amounts of damage –
some £50 million each year. However,
scientists warn that if you disturb the balance...'

[Somehow it seems a long way back to me:
the swollen, mucoid features, bulging, blind;
the conjured image, furry, indistinct;
the dim, projected concept in poor light;
the corrupt corpses of the unfortunate
(we are all members of the Wildlife Trust)
viewed through an ancient epidiascope;
the deluded ramblings of Old Ma Hope.]

From the Chinese

*'The Sage's words
are untranslatable.'*
ANON.

He is a mock sportsman
who slings a dead rat
in his girdle.

He who has
an iron mouth
and bean-curd feet
will not be able
to escape trouble.

He who does not drink
has a negligible wine bill.

Soap (*I.M.*, G.E.)

Joey is outraged at Pacey's advance
but starts to question her reaction.
Henry disappoints Jen by not inviting her to his birthday,
while Tricia makes Marlon's day
and Rosa has an angry confrontation
with Fiona Morris. Gianni, on the other hand,
gets some devastating news from his solicitor.
Meanwhile, Fraser is forced to take drastic action
against his ruthless new landlord and Jamie
hits back at Billy.

                    But – what's this?!:
Tad gets mad with Paul and Simone
and, before you know where you are,
Mandy visits her dad,
Joel's courting ends in calamity,
Roy is furious to find out
about Scott's underhand dealings
and Bernice questions Zoe's commitment,
so of course Geoff and Doreen
catch Jack and Vera out
and Linda tries desperately
to conceal the truth about Mike's health
even though Tad holds a grudge against Paul and Simone
and Pollard threatens to expose Scott
and the next thing you know is
Danny steams ahead with his plans
to marry the girl of his dreams,
Joe is not happy that Flick played truant,
Ashley considers a shock proposal,
Chris makes plans with Tara's money,
Zak and Cain lay down the law,
Tony is annoyed that Adam stayed the night,
Tim makes things worse for Sinbad,
Mick has a romantic proposition for Susannah,
Felicity stands her ground with Sean,

Joel struggles with his feelings for Dione
(Emily is frankly appalled),
a journalist looks for Nicky di Marco,
Dan continues to harass Melanie
which leads Steve into taking some drastic action,
Tricia realises the truth about Marlon,
Gary embarks on a holiday romance,
Darren is evicted
and the whole fucking schemozzle
ends in a welter of puke, shite and claret.

In Glen Waverley, Melbourne,

over High Street Road, where rush-hour
lasts twenty hours a day
and the pantechnicons hurtle
and honk through exhaust-fume smog,

up on the giant lamp-posts
above the rage of the traffic
a bunch of Sulphur-crested
Cockatoos overwhelms
the din with harridan skreeches.

And one wonders what early settlers
made of the murderous screams
coming out of virgin forest
where they landed, fearing the worst.

Emission

The Plant disperses plenty no good shit –

sulphuric hailstones drub your washing-lines,
acidulate your long johns, jumpers, jeans.

Faunal

I

...who sat on the rail
nursing a Smith & Wesson *Chief's Special.*

With the percussion,
dove backwards
into the cleanliness of the weir.

[Let us regard with compassionate resign
those unfortunates whom
we shall assuredly join.]

II

If you woke up x hundred years ago,
on a spring morning such as this, maybe
you'd be inclined to conjour in your mind:

What maketh thus this Sparrowy Tribe to twitter?!

III

Looking over the rail
of the fish wharf, Monterey Harbour:
immediately below was a Southern Sea Otter
(Enhydra lutris nereis)
crunching a crab, between bites
resting it on its chest.

Later, at Point Lobos,
another of those remarkable creatures,
this time bashing Mussels to bits
on its chest on a stone anvil which it clutched to
each time it dived
to wrest another mollusc
from the rocks under the floating brown Kelp...

Inconsequential, maybe,
but I have a dead friend
whom I recall on these occasions.

IV

Again the Homeric dream,
Olive and Oleaster,
under which the fallen leaves are scraped
and demise commences.

At Pelee Point

It was decorous that day, Johnston, my friend, to slosh out the vintage
(the Pelee Island white with its label adroitly depicting
a Great Blue Heron) and raise our generous golden bumpers
to the Bald Eagle, American Woodcock, Scarlet Tanager,
Bay-breasted, Chestnut-sided and Blackburnian Warblers,
and commit ourselves to the onset of the autumn migration.

[Untitled]

The small skiff has been rowed
deep into the Great Reed-mace,
the oars are stowed,
the occupant deadly supine
in the clinker planks,
a Bittern, mottled dead-bracken,
bill erect, static, *whoomp-booms*,
and there is autumnal evening precipitation.

Axiomatic

The Sage seems ridiculous
            to the eighth-rate twerp.

                    Comfort and warmth
            are conducive to love;
                    hunger and cold
            to theft and thuggery.

Reiterative

   Now, beyond hope, I still owe the gods great gratitude.
Marvels are many, mankind among them who navigates oceans,
driven by stormy south-westers, making way through the billows
and surges that threaten to drown and engulf his laborious progress.
And Earth, wearied, wears on, each year turning under the plough.

[Untitled]

Tanker founders,
on slick-black holiday sands
oiled auks flacker.

Brr...

When the telephone
stridently pierces the dark:
'Did I love my Mom enough?
Whaddabout my Pop?'

Those *Alligator mississippiensis*

delicately copulating in a lagoon
in Aransas, south-east Texas,
their fondling, fumbling under
the surface with sensual claws
and jaws, the joyous writhing
needs neither intellectual
nor moral smartarse envoi.

[Untitled]

In the Library
all seem to have some *purpose*.
I, *per contra*, plot
a visit to the NatWest,
followed by intemperance.

Axiomatic

We take off our shoes;
will we wear them tomorrow?

We can't foretell this morning
what will befall this evening.

When we go to bed
we cannot be sure that we
will rise tomorrow.

When the black leech sticks
to the foot of the egret
he struggles to shake it off
but is unable.

Up in the Chiricahuas,

about 9,000 feet,
a switchback trail through spruce
and pine to a beat-up fire-lookout,
Steller's Jay, Pygmy Nuthatch,
Mexican Chickadee,
impeccable Red-faced Warbler...

Later, *vinum sacrum*
to properly honour this day
of secular *epiphania*.

Port Fairy,

Victoria,
the only mainland colony
of Short-tailed Shearwaters,
dusk before they bullet,
from the day's pelagic foraging,
into the coney burrows
to regurgitate their piscine
mulch in the gapes of fledglings,
no longer at risk from diurnal
predation.

They are silent
as, an inch above our heads,
close enough to ruffle
our hair, their ballistic shades
hurtle towards the fish stink.

Well, we won't experience *that* again in a hurry –
notch it up, therefore, Deborah, while you may.

Bird Lady

Under a pine in Vondelpark
the Bird Lady has fashioned
an impromptu feed-table,
arrives each morning laden
with bags of sunflower seeds
and kibbled maize and proceeds
to feed the feral Rose-rings
(Psittacula krameri,
40 centimetres,
general plumage green,
yellowish underwing,
in male, rose collar encircling
hindneck, nape suffused
bluish) and Alexandrines
(Psittacula eupatria,
58 centimetres,
a group of pristine males,
occiput and cheeks
suffused with bluish-grey,
black stripe through lower cheek,
pink collar encircling hindneck,
red slash on secondary coverts,
massive vermilion bill,
call – a skreeching *kee-ak),*
which, were it not for her
genial dottiness,
would not survive the severe
calorie-wasting winter,
and *we* would be undernourished.

That Nine-banded Armadillo

(Dasypus novemcinctus)
scruttering into the brush
and Prickly Pear of a pathside
in Aransas, south-east Texas,
requires no fancy moral
or intellectual envoi.

In Victoria

When the rafts of Little Penguins
(Eudyptula minor) ascend
through the punishing surf of the ocean
to the Philip Island colony
as the safety of darkness arrives
and they burst from the water and flapper
up to the occupied burrows
where the waiting nestlings clamour
there is laughter and condescension
and the flashing of Nikons and Canons
from the vapid goons who have gathered
to gawp from their raked terrace seats.

Field Note (Everglades)

As elevated nostrils
and eye sockets
of an *Alligator mississippiensis*
slow-motion cruise
across the black channel
a Green Heron
(Butorides virescens)
which has remained fixed
leaning precarious to the water
for fifteen minutes precisely
edges back along its twig
with the choreographed dexterity
of a survivor.

Journal

Of primitive creatures I observed a few,
after we landed at St Jago – large
Aplysia are common. This sea-slug,
grey-yellow coloured, has two antennae
in shape resembling some mammal's ears.
Each side the long foot there's a wide membrane
which, rippling, causes water currents to flow
over the dorsal branchiae.

                              It feeds
on fragile matter. I found in its gut
all sorts of festering slurry. When 'tis jabbed,
this slug emits a purplish fluid, also
stinging secretions rendering it repulsive.

I found, in the same place, *H. sapiens.*

I found, in one part, this grave malady:
General Paralysis of the Insane –
outdated term for tertiary syphilis.

Becalmed, next day, in a *Sargassum* limbo.

One time we passed the night in Punta Alta,
busied myself with palaeontology.
An evening of perfection, calm and clear,
mud-banks and gulls, sandhills, suspended vultures.

I found no fossil but my single self.

We saw a couple of *Zorillas*, or skunks –
odious creatures, far from uncommon here.
They roam by day about the open plain
fearing nor dog nor man, their fetid fluid
inducing nausea and rendering those
polluted by it useless everafter.

Azara says the stink can be discerned
at a league's distance – more than once, indeed,
on the entering of Monte Video Harbour,
breeze being offshore, we have olfactoried it
aboard the vessel. Certainty it is
that even Man rates poor with the *Zorilla*
in this respect of fundamental stench.

When the bull has been dragged to the slaughterplace,
the *matador*, with caution, slashes the hamstrings.
That death-bellow is a sound more eloquent
than any ferocious agony I know.

The struggle now is drawing to a close:
this earth comprises bones and blood; the horses
and riders wallow in gore/faeces slough.

During my sojourn in Bahia Blanca,
awaiting the arrival of our vessel,
three hundred men arrived from the Colorado
under command of Commandant Miranda.

Most of these men were *mansos* Indians
who passed the night here. 'Tis impossible
to conceive of anything more odious
than the hideous vision of their bivouac:
some drank unto profound intoxication;
some gulped the still-steaming blood of slaughtered cattle,
then, vomiting from drunkenness, cast up,
smirching themselves with puke and filthy gore.

Of the Batrachian reptiles, I discovered
only one tiny toad, most singular
in colouration – if we imagine, first,
that it was steeped in blackest ink, and then,
when dry, had been allowed to crawl across
a board fresh-painted bright vermilion,
so as to tint its soles and underbelly,
some notion of its appearance may be gained.

If no nomenclature has been yet applied,
then, surely, it should be *diabolicus*,
for 'tis a toad to preach in the ear of Eve.

Our sleeping place was the Lagoa Marcia.
We passed, at dusk, under a granite steepness
(so common hereabouts) and this terrain
had been for many years the residence
of runaway slaves, who managed to cultivate
a little land atop, and eke a subsistence.

At length they were discovered, and, a posse
of soldiers being sent, the whole were seized,
with th' exception of one old crone, who, rather than
submit herself again to slavery,
dashed herself into pieces from the crag.

After we took fresh vegetables aboard,
December 1833, our vessel
sailed from the Rio Plata, nevermore
to enter its Stygian waters, for Patagonia.
We were infested with insects. As we headed
one evening ten miles off the Bay of San Blas,
vast numerous hordes of butterflies appeared,
far as the telescope could range, and they all drowned.
The sailors cried: 'This is impossible!
'Tis snowing butterflies!' I'm told the species
was *Colias edusa*. I am indebted
to Waterhouse for the naming of these dead.

The deathly stillness of that plain, those dogs

guarding the gipsy tribe of Gauchos, sleeping
beside their campfire, have left in my mind
a memory not soon to be forgotten.

And of all things I've seen and thought and done,
this voyage was my most remarkable.

*

I riffle my notebooks' leaves now at my desk
(they seem to have been laid down so long ago,
like palaeontological deposits) –

'On Chatham Island, I slept one night on shore.
Next morning, glowing heat. I scrambled over
the rough volcanic surface of the ground,
which, taken with the intricacy of barbed thickets,
served to fatigue me greatly. I was amply
rewarded by a strange Cyclopean scene.
Two huge tortoises, each of which, if weighed,
must have been in excess of 200 pounds.
One of them masticated on a cactus,
and, as I drew close, paused to examine me,
then quietly walked away; the other hissed
before withdrawing into its carapace.
The sheer size of these reptiles, their stark context,
surrounded by black lava, leafless shrubs,
and spiky cacti, they seemed, to my fancy,
like creatures roused from antediluvian sleep...'

I riffle my notebooks' leaves now at my desk –

one page is gnarled and stained from salt spray hurled
by the Humboldt Current onto laval rocks:

And I muse on origins and extirpations.

Endangered

Down on the Gulf Coast of Texas, in the Aransas wetland,
   Johnston and I were observing a posse of Whooping Cranes
(*Grus americana*), Titanium White in crisp focus
    through the Bausch & Lomb, red facial skin, black primaries,
    and a Goddam wingspan of eighty-seven inches.
When they took flight, the trumpets sounded over the marshes,
kerloo kerleeloo, kerloo kerleeloo, kerloo kerleeloo,
and we knew, we knew we would die without seeing the species again.

[Untitled]

Costa del Parvenu:
plenty of foil,
plenty of melanomas.

Laertidean

Drove to the Holy Island over the
    salt-caked causey,
where there were Eiders, Bar-tailed Godwits,
    pale-bellied Brent Geese.
High on the gale-lashed crags above nineteenth-
    century lime-kilns,
Fulmars were nesting: tubular nostrils,
    bull-necks, stiff-winged
gliding and beating. Launching from ledges, they
    lifted, effortless.

And we considered Cuthbert, who, in his
    youth was a sheep herd,
went there as Abbot, then Biscop, and later
    lived as an eremite.
Dane-hordes threatened the monks of Lindisfarne,
    Cuthbert was borne far –
lies now in Durham Cathedral. And we con-
    sidered the crinoids,
Beads of Saint Cuthbert, encrinite fossils.
    And we considered.

of Peleus' son's wrath
I venture to speak

Zeus willed it
but the expedition
caused such grief
with many fine warriors
consigned to the soil

Muse relate how first was engendered the Great Quarrel

the forces were displayed
then were they gathered
each several squadron
all breathing valour

then I the Sacker of Cities
rose up and routed them

then Pandarus broke the truce
then did red-haired Menelaus
rouse his ranks to courage

then did Diomedes war with the Gods
then did the battle-shields' clash continue endless

then Hector bellowed a battle-cry causing the
    Argives to tremble
then he seized up a huge rock from under the massive
    gates of the ramparts
and it tapered into a spear-sharp point
    and its weight was such
that any *ten* men in these enfeebled
    times couldn't raise it
yet for Hector this boulder seemed merely a pebble
    he lifted it lightly
and he braced his legs for a powerful throw
    and he flexed his muscles
then hurtled the missile into the doors which were
    strengthened with stout bars
and the hinges burst and he leapt inside and his
    brow was night-black
then the son of Priam rallied his forces to
    let slip the war-dogs

Then I came to a cottage of stone
at the southern foot of the Long Mynd,
and the masonry's fossils conveyed,
in runes of deposited crinoids
and Silurian brachiopods,
the unending unnerving axiom,
the unending unnerving axiom...

and against the walls a vine thrived,
clustered with generous grapes,
and from its five-fingered leaves
she fondly made me dolmas
with olives and rice and spiced meat,
and we drained red wine and reclined
and I recollected Achilles
and the mists veiling Ilion's ramparts,
and on my departure I heaved
an *Oimoi!* for what I was losing.

then the bellicose Hector threatened our ships and
    huts as he ventured

    seaward through our
    Argive encampment

slaughtering all in his path but he met the
    mass of our forces

when the Achaeans countered him brandishing
    two-spike spear-heads

then the aggressor fell back but with volume
    called on his quailing

troops to return to the warfield – Ilians
Lycians also Dardanians (noted for
    hand-to-hand combat)

though Achaeans stood thick as wall-stones Hector
thought he could rout our armies perforce
since he was sent by the Thunder-One Master of Hērē

so we then slew the captured Dolon
    son of Eumedes
after he'd given us good information
    concerning the Thracians
where they were camped and of their magnificent
    snow-white horses
and we threaded our way through the sable night till we
    found them sleeping
with their priceless gear by their sides and their bold mounts
    tethered beside them
and Rhesus their king in their centre asleep
    with his steeds and his chariot
then the son of Tydeus inspired by Athene and
    wielding his bright blade
slaughtered the slumbering forces from Thrace where they lay

By Amtrak out of Austin to Alpine,
couple of iced Buds in the rattling bar
followed by T-bone and Fort Stockton red.
And through the dust-grained window of the Club Car,
pink Scissor-tails migrating with the fall
and vultures southbound for the borderline
and dried-up gulches, and the tender said:
'I bin this rowt, now, twenny years an all;
nothin much happens in th desert har,
save for th casional flowrin prickly par
an flash-floods thro th dra creek over thar –
I guess ya could say…' but he never finished.
The arid basin, with our speed, diminished;
the glass revealed a season in decline.

Then I sailed | to the Isle | of the Saint | who had shipped |
long ago | with Saint Bren | dan the bold | and his age |
I was told | was two hun | dred-and-twen | ty-five years |
and he spake | in the tones | of a soul | from the kist |
who was one | with the blithe | and his glance | was serene |
and his hair | which was frost | and his beard | which was snow |
were a me | tre in mea | sure and more | and he judged |
that my peo | ple have feu | ded too long | and entrea- |
ted we pon | der the words | of the Lord | who said Ven- |
gance is Mine! | and he railed | how our fa | thers have slain |
and been slain | life for life | interne | cine and *when* |
will the hom | icide cease? | and we knelt | at the fringe |
of his beard | and we prayed | and we prayed | and we prayed. |

then while the son of Tydeus
like a lion on the sheepfold
slew a dozen more men of Thrace
I snatched each one by the foot
and unceremoniously flung it
out of the path of the long-maned
stallions we wanted to plunder
and I untethered the thoroughbreds
and tied them together with thongs
and led them away from the blood-field
and upon Athene's advice
we made off for our Argive vessels

and when Hector observed our mighty warrior Patroclus
limp from the fray gouting gore he thrust his bronze spear
    deep through the guts of the son
    of Menoetius of Opus
then the slaying of Priam's son by Achilles was foretold
but Hector scoffed and trod on the fallen Achaean
    and wrenchèd his brazen spear-spike
    out of the corpse's chitterling
and the cadaver soon slipped off the lance and landed
      with its face upwards
      then ensued more wrath

Then we waded at low tide to Hilbre Island;/and we marvelled at scores of thousands of waders – / Sanderling, Knot, Oystercatcher, Redshank, Curlew and Dunlin;/and the giant gull of the north, the hyperborean Glaucous,/glided snow-mantled above the remains of the old lifeboat station;/and there suddenly stooped from a cloud the colour of Blaenau Ffestiniog slate/a Peregrine into a blizzard of wheeling *Calidris alba*/and the falcon hit and we heard the thud and a handful of silvern feathers/whorled in the wind and the great dark raptor rose with the dead meat locked in its talons;/and I said to my friend: 'We will mind this as long as we live.' (He is dead now.)

then each of the Danaan leaders
    ferociously slaughtered his foe
they harried the Trojans just as a ravenous pack
    of wolves does a sheepfold of lambs
snatching the innocents fresh from beneath their ewes' bellies
    whenever the negligent shepherd
abandons his timid charges thus the Danaans
    dealt with the Ilian hordes
    scattering them into rout

Landed on Ynys Enlli, island of
  currents, where we re-

garded a number of myxomatosic
  leporids, mirroring

hominid exit (slime-swollen, tumoral)
  in the next shit-show –

    which, you with certainty know,
    will not be very long now.

then Agamemnon took on Peisander and
    bold Hippolochus

then Atreus' son speared Peisander deeply
    splintring the sternum

then he sworded Hippolochus' arms then the second
    son of Antimachus'
head like a round rock rolled through the awed mob

and I recall how brash Diomedes
    fought with the Gods his
battle-skreech cowed even Aphrodite
    daughter of Great Zeus

and how her lovely skin was incarnadine
when with Iris she left to the left of the field of slaughter

Touched down, Beograd:
slivovitz, crno vino –
   heady days, before
Milosovic rose enraged,
raved and deracinated.

Thence to the Bay of Chesapeake's stubble-fields,
Johnston and I, binoculars tremulous,
    scanning the hoared-land blacked with *Brantas*
    and, in their centre, a single Snow Goose.

then Hector's hurled spear shied off Achilles' shield

the Trojan's body was guarded by bright bronze
yet the Achaean felled our foe with a long lance through the gullet

Landed, at last, among friends;
there in the land I belonged.

Then I regained mine own Penelope.

Afflatious

That cinnamon Nankeen Night Heron
(slender, white nuchal plumes,
black crown, black bill, cream belly)
at roost on an island willow
brushing the brown lake mirror
in Melbourne Botanical Gardens...

And in Texas, that Painted Bunting
(head purple, back green, rump red,
red underparts, dark wings and tail,
bizarrely designed by committee)
picking at tumblegrass seed
in our arid desert garden...

And on Bardsey, off the Welsh coast,
that Wryneck (*Jynx torquilla*)
we caught in the mist-nets, beating
between the bracken and gorse clumps –
the way its head twisted around,
serpentine, primitive,
its vermicular dead-leaf plumage...

And in Badgers Creek, that Lyre Bird
(*Menura novaehollandiae*),
grey-brown, long filmentous tail,
and feet like a couple of garden rakes
grubbing the wet forest leaf-mould...

And on the Mexican border,
that Plain Chachalaca, dull grey,
long glizy green tail tipped white,
guzzling the leaves from the branches,
cha–cha–lac, cha–cha–lac, cha–cha–lac...

And I'd say (if I entertained
such mawkish conceits) that on each

of these afflatious encounters
my soul ascended like that
Skylark I watched as I lay
and dreamed through a summer morning
in a sweet pasture in Shropshire
on an upland when I was younger.

CIVIL

(2002)

Prince Rupert's Cavaliers being victors here,
we and the town was subject to their pillage,
they then possessed our very homes and lives,
damning and cursing, threatening, frightening
our womenfolk with naked blades and pistols,
they picked our purses, sought out any wealth
they thought we might have hid in outhouses
and any other place they could suppose
we had concealed our modest stores and savings.
We was compelled thus to yield goods and money,
our women being robbed of chastity,
their impudent molesters bragging of it,
boasting of their lascivious lechery.
That night the plunderers did not retire,
but sat up revelling, robbing and raping.
Next day, with gunpowder and stooks of straw,
they fired our humblest hovels for their sport.

In sorrow shalt thou bring forth children here.

Your brother's blood shall shriek from the fresh clay.

Who sheds blood shall have blood shed [and ad inf.].

Life/life, eye/eye, hand/hand, foot/foot, tooth/tooth,
incendiary/incendiary [ad inf.].

And, Lo!, there was a great cry down in Egypt
[and, yea, in this sectarian, scepter'd isle].

In howling waste aridity swords smote.

Then did Jael Heber's wife pull out a tent-nail,
then did she raise in her right hand a hammer,
then did she creep upon her sleeping foe,
then did she smite the spike deep through his brain.

Then Saul slew thousands, David tens of thousands.

My name is Thomas Tasker, labourer,
of Epwell, Oxfordshire, being an old, poor man.
On one December middle of the night
in 1644, a rowdy group
of Major Purefoy's Parliamentarian troops
came to this house and violently possessed
the most part of our household goods, about
£10 or more in value, and seized me
and bore me off to Compton without charge
where I was jailed for six days, when this Major
came to me with harsh speeches and gave order
that I should be released, but never asked me
of any supposed crime, nor would he give
me any leave to speak for myself or ask
for any of my goods to be returned.

This sudden fright has made me and my wife
so sickly and so weak, we are unable
to make our living.

           The soldiers took away
ten shillings money, seven pairs of sheets,
two brass pots, divers pewter,
four shirts, four smocks and other linen items,
two coats, one cloak, one waistcoat, seven dozen
of candles, a peck of wheat, four bags of oatmeal,
a frying pan, a spit, two pairs of pot hooks,
a basket full of eggs, pins, bowls and dishes,
spoons, ladles, drinking pots, all they could carry.

Then Hector bellowed forth a battle-cry,
the Argives trembled, he ripped up a rock,
far greater than *ten* men could raise today,
and hurled it at the iron-bracèd gate –

the hinges burst and he let forth a roar,
and all was mayhem, as had been before

(and was to be at Naseby, Marston Moor...).

Oi ad eleven orses as wus took
by the King's soldiers – four they orses, mind,
wus worth full forty pounds. Oi ad anuvver
nine took an Oi never seed em agin.

One day weem orf t market wiv the corn,
they soldiers of the Earl o Manchester
met us an took the ole durnd team o drays.

They King's fine soldiers labels me a Roundyod;
Parlyment's soldiers says Oi pays me rent
to Royalist Worcester. Oi, though, for meself,
conna tell rightly what theym om about –
Oi only knows Oi lorst me corn an orses.

The 'Sealed Knot' boys and girls are here in Ludlow
puerilely playing Cavaliers and Roundheads,
Brigadier Bashforth-Shellingem in command.
The castle is assaulted and insulted,
and when they've biffed each other on the Field
(the blanks, the smoke, the kiddy-swords and cannons)
they 'hie them' (quaint that, ain't it?) to Chris's pub
where they require 'Real Ale' in beer-buff bumpers.

(And, furthermore, they think it's all O.K.,
they think it's all O.K., they think that shit.)

Anceftral yobberie doth yet preuail;
ciuil hoftilitie is atauiftic:

In Ludlow, after ten generations, still,
I'm happy to report, the Smiths and Bradleys
knock shit out of each other Saturday nights.

'Pray God send peace,' he groaned at last, 'or else
I see that which will come to this land quickly.'

(2003)

'The Marginal Mark for *Delete?!* –
this time he *is* pushing his luck!'

This obfusc forest
(no longer the midst of life),
    the course, of course, lost.

In the tavern of Cristóval:
raucous music;
good people, their voices *ronco*;
cristal – goblet-glint of good wine,
glint-bright pane onto the Market Place,
lens of the eye,
lens of the eye.

And, in the tavern of Cristóval,
considerations that engender transient *coplas*.

In the tavern of Cristóval
consider the news of your new-dead mentor,
recall the fecund estuary,
the happy island –
field ornithology loses a limb
as today, here,
you re-read this sad, unwelcome epistle,
here, in the tavern of Cristóval.

276

A spectrum sphere, child's blown bubble,
incongruously wafts past a window
of the Globe where we imbibe while we may;

a bewildered sparrow flackered through
the fleeting vigour of a once great mead-hall.

Pendulous-globed vine girdles the wall-angle,
there is fragrant oleaginous lavender,
rosemary, mint, laurel –

it was good, while it lasted.

In this Market Place,
white eggs,
white lilies for the cadaver,
schmaltz watercolours depicting defunct rusticity,
atavistic tweed duds,
in this Market Place.

And, in this Market Place,
redundant kickshaws –
a busted butter-churn,
tarnished trash-trinkets,
gold, silver, brass, base metal,
cracked bourgeois crocks,
world's gear,
world's gear,
world's gear...
in this Market Place.

And, in this Market Place,
Stark Mortality,
offer you can't refuse,
in this Market Place.

No, there is nothing, no thing,
after the planting or pyre...

What you achieved (if you *did*)
is your own conscience's fret.

The Great Hall,
the men at the *medubenc*,
the disoriented *Passer domesticus*
fluttering fleetingly through,
the honeyed beakerfuls,
the *Scop*,
the harp's strike,
the *Hwaet!*,
the powerful *sang*,
the consideration of mortality.

Well, callow wet-eared whelp, you presume to
        come to advise *us*?,
    Junior Real-Estate Clerk?,
    dishing the clichés and bull?:

basically, *at the end of the day*, and the
        deeply-dreadeds –
    bottom-line, *hopefully*...? Well,
    fuck the hell off outa here.

    Dusk falls: young girls,
    water-chestnut
    gatherers, pass;

an old Calligrapher
    (moon frosts his room)
    confronts a page
    stubbornly blank.

Many malign pestiferous phlegm-slimes
writhed in this vile reptilian seething mass,
the stench of which induced faeces and vomit
(my chitterling voids, e'en now, to recollect,
until I swoon in etiolated terror).

Noosed in these scaled constrictuous twisting coils,
the naked vulnerable shrieked their spasms –
genitals gimleted by *Ophidia*
which exited from assholes, tied tight knots,
inflicted mass excoriating torture.

My Guide to me: 'Observe the eternal lot
of *sapiens*, whether he transgress or not.'

This Sixth Molar,
molested unmercifully
by years' ravages,
abstract it, Dentist, please –
first bit of the whole foul heap
to go for good.

Poor parasite: you require Valerius' *lucrum* to live on?
  Gaius replies: you will die talentless, virtueless, broke.

¿That viejo,
dentro de Mesón Cristóval,
contiguo escaparate,
bebedor, bebedor?,

¿he has much tristeza, sí?,
¿he has aflicción?,
¿some troubles of dinero?

No, he is cansado,
viejo, simplemente.

Sir Edward Elgar
scribbled his Pomp & Circ. No.5
on the back of an Ordnance Survey map
while he was out for a drive
in the English countryside...

Those Elysian days
(of course it was *all* fields *then*)
when to purchase petrol
seemed not to be a culpable offence...

That Worcestershire,
that pellucid Severn,
that remnant of rurality,
that Nation,
that notion,
that Empire,
that frail hurtling thing third from Helios...

Oars of smoothed pine polished white by the waves of
    oceans shattered –
those of my crew whom I valued most were
    plucked from the gunwales
shrieking the names of their kindred as they
    hurtled gulfwards
(just as a skilful angler using a
    sliver of ox-horn
filed to a barbed hook casts out the glinting
    lure towards small fry,
tweaking them into the rocks to perish
    pounded and broken;
so were my boldest brothers snatched from their
    transient safety).

I have endured much on the whipped brine but
    never such raw grief.

    In irriguous terraces
new-planted, loved, delicate shoots thrive,
    ripen, are sickled, dried, threshed...

    The cauldron takes the yield's-end.

In the tavern of Cristóval,
those of us seeking the cure
(the maladies are divers –
do not name them, for we all know, we all know...)
assemble daily, daily to drain, to drain...

And from the window
of the tavern of Cristóval,
we view the comfy, complacent carpetbaggers
from the big tax-zones, early-retired,
fucking up the real-estate
for the indigenous, impecunious honest.

And outside the tavern of Cristóval,
they think that it's O.K., that it's O.K.

That trumpet-rattle of Sandhill Cranes,
   audible over a mile –
   soon you will be deaf to it.

Here, in Bolivia,
I chisel the racked body,
plane the crude effigy,
   here in Bolivia;
and where *real* iron nails
spurt the bright *sangre* from sapped palms,
from drained foot-veins,
   here in Bolivia
I splatter bright carmine right from the tube;
   and here, in Bolivia,
I spear with violence the side,
the deep bloody gash spiked with *real* cold steel,
gore from *my* raw hands
stains the abused places
   here in Bolivia;
real thorns and *my* head's blood
befoul His face,
and the Nazarene bleeds
   here, now, in Bolivia.

Down in what seemed to me the deepmost slime-pit
they slithered like dead meat in a foetid broil.

My Guide to me: 'These are mere men and women
whose crime was recklessly to have been born.'

Men at the *medubenc*!, meditate:

myrige, maybe, while *sumor* lasts
with *fugol-sang*;
but now, winds blast,
weder beats, defeats;
even a king becomes subject,

when tides fare fair – to the *medubenc*!;
when tides fare foul – to the *medubenc*!

Somebody mentioned that Caesar's mother had 'passed in her slumbers'.
Not bad – one-hundred-and-one years without shifting one's arse.

A track switchbacked above the Malebolge
to where an arch of cast-iron-coloured granite
bridged a black chasm of unplumbable depth
from which vile stenches, slurpings, porcine snorts
rose, redolent of rank faecal cesspit slurry,
and dimly through the gloom of that abyss
the Mantuan unfolded to my poor vision
humankind wallowing in its feculent filth,
shite-spattered, splutt'ring gobs of diarrhoea,
then breathed this one word, *sotto voce*: 'You.'

He is reading to his wife:
approaching the fiction's end,
    he decelerates –
who does not regret last lines?

And the evening and the morning were the first day

But there went up a mist from the Plant
which acidulated the land

In sorrow shall thou bring forth children

The voice of your brother's blood
shall shrill from fresh loam

Who sheds blood shall have blood shed [*ad inf*]

Life/life eye/eye molar/molar
hand/hand foot/foot incendiary/incendiary

And there was a great cry in Egypt [and here
there and yea everywhere]

In the howling waste aridity

Smote
sword

Then did Jael Heber's wife pull a nail from the tent-ropes
then did she raise up a mallet
then did she creep on her sleeping foe
then did she smite the spike deep through his brain pan

Then Saul slew thousands
David tens of thousands

Fiat Lux

Defunct calligraphist,
white page stubbornly blank.
Nothing more, nothing more.

May *morwening*
when lanes are cream-clotted
with hawthorn, cow parsley,
when blush apple blossom
    flocks rich orchards,
    consider this:

it is nearly finished –
next year?, the year after?

'Those were the days!', you say? Mneah! –
out of Commencement came Kleiō
to fettle us, fuck up our Fate.

Twenty years are gone from me,
fighting mad Dynastic wars.
　　Today, I return:
all is abandoned, house sacked,
garden weed-rife, wife AWOL.

Again, dread dreams
(so many, these nights) –
my father, mother,
brother, all there, there.!

The Mantovan's glare –
cold-sculpted eyeballs
bare of irises...

Marble drapery,
all, all frost marble...

My Guide to me: 'Observe,
Time's-Wreak,
Time's-Wreak,
Time's-Wreak...'

This morning he scrawled
one Haiku of no merit.

This falling darkness:

that of which he is able
is a failed Tanka only.

As Artemis or golden Aphrodite,
Penelope shone there on his return.

[But men age quickly in adversity.]

Mister, we are worse than the excrement of hogs
(which does nothing wrong,
but only enriches the earth),
for we crack on rocks the backs
of our fucking stupid supertankers
(which we dispatch
despite our retrospective intelligence),
and thereby, for reasons of avarice,
precipitate extirpation.

Today, once more,
extirpation...

Well, Mister, as I have elsewhere remarked,
it is a fucking good job
that it all doesn't matter.

Dirges of viols:
Reading is dead,
Reading is dead;
reading remains.

In the tavern of Cristóval
many are there who have good lives;
many are there who have *tristeza*...

nevertheless,
in the tavern of Cristóval
all, all assemble daily.

You, whom I choose to dismiss in a distich, satisfied now, eh?
Take Gaius' *sesterces*, yes; what you *can't* have is his skill.

We have ditched most of the draff:
the unbidden spineless books,
the grot-gathering gubbins,
the outvogued vestments,
the cracked crockery,
the pot pig moneybox,
the Morecambe Bay mug,
the vintner's final demand,
the last but one's divorce papers,
the last home's deeds,
the chimp's wizened scrotum souvenir,
world's gear,
the bulk of the whole fucking shitheap.

That which remains is a cleared desk
and a time of appointment.

My Guide to me:
'This subfusc *flumen*,
    so soon traversed,
may not be recrossed.'

Astrophysicists,
carbon-daters,
compositors,
morticians
and snow-haired chirographists know

blank space is integral to the whole.

Then the warrior-king, red-haired Menelaus,
    said to Telemachus:

Well, if you wish, then of course return
    to your father's fastness,

though I must tell you, three things are the
    duties of nobles –

first, a guest should be treated with honour
    while he is fêted;

second, a guest who must go should not be de-
    tained by some over-

sedulous shelterer (no one should be claustro-
    phobically clinging);

third, fine food and riches should swell the de-
    parter's chariot

(white-armed, high-born Helen will fettle spiced
    meats from our kitchens,

there must be wine, and, of course, this mixing-bowl
    wrought by Hephaestus…).

    Thus should a man take his leave;
    suitably sated, equipped.

Señor, you ask me the route to Xalapa?
I tell you, Señor, that at this crossroads
one way may be a good route;
the other way may be a bad route.
Similarly, Señor,
one way may be a bad route;
the other way may be a good route.

My father, he lived in Xalapa;
my mother, she lived also in Xalapa;
there, also, my predecessors, all, all...

I tell you, Señor,
the destination is the same, the same.

We give them fresh-cut willow-sprigs
    when dear friends leave
our modest hospitality;

    nevertheless,
how we sigh on their departure.

That of which *H. sap.* is capable is no longer surprising.

[These were the words of the auspex: *Inter-
necine destruction...*]

TV breaks the shit
(Christianity,
Mahometism...);
we sit relishing
gold wine – *ars brevis.*

I salute you, Californian
William Johnston, whom I can't repay

since that time of Phainopepla
in the desert scrubland, Joshua way,

since, in that oasis verdure:
Verdin, Costa's Hummer, Hooded Oriole...

#

Fellow-Toper/Field-Guide-Wielder,
now, before the final fucking toll,

I, with catalectic trochees, try to get
somewhere near to clearing off my greatest debt.

Dawn's lume,
bakers' ovens' fragrance:

new bread –
we live for one day more.

Herewith, a deep-delv'd draught to *Luscinia*
    megarhynchos...

but it wasn't *jug-jug* I heard that night on the
    outskirts of Mostar,

night of torrential rain, before the
    bridge was bisected,

it was a cadence of ominous harmony
    not to be heard since,

and *was* forlorn, and the very sound seemed,
    yes, like a tolling.

Outside, the Big Superstitions rage.

In this transiently snug kitchen,
pigeon breasts casseroled in Languedoc
   and our own grapes.

Fall; our table is already laid –
   vines adorn it.

   Soon, nettle soup.

In your nightmare, you and I descend;
I stride towards us, unblinking,
unrecognising, and pass.

ˎ

From leaf-mould-moist copses:

Veery ⎫
Swainson's ⎬ throstle-fugol-sang...
Hermit ⎪
Wood . ⎭

well, as you do us,
we hymn y'all

until *all* voices silence
until   voices silence
until   silence
un

That which you do
do with circumspection
and consider extirpation.

INDEX OF TITLES & FIRST LINES

(Titles are shown in italics, first lines in roman type.
Untitled poems are indexed under first lines only.)

Two new words today, 44

Under a dripping Yew, a sandstone tablet, 180
Under a pine in Vondelpark, 229
Unfortunately, 57
[untitled], 147-200
[untitled] poems: look under first lines
Up in the Chiricahuas, 227

Vast tracts of shit have yet to be discovered, 86
Veracruz ('A colony of Howler Monkeys'), 85
Veracruz ('A dirt road furrowed and flooded'), 58
Veracruz ('October evening'), 63
Veracruz ('Outside the village'), 51
Victoria, 228

Wake, dull brain, and contemplate this, 52
We anchored in a bay under the island, 209
We give them fresh-cut willow-sprigs, 301
We have ditched most of the draff, 297
We take off our shoes, 227
we were driving along a dirt road, 203
Well, callow wet-eared whelp, you presume to, 280
What a wonderful row, 29
When supermarkets open at 8 a.m., 62
When the gipsy Preciosa, 166
When the rafts of Little Penguins, 230
When the telephone, 225
When we arrived at the stubble fields dawn hadn't, 61
When you playfully, 60
Whenever I whiff, 60
Where *gravitas* nor levity can stir him, 92
...who sat on the rail, 221
With each dawn, 156
With *sol.* it means scholastic disputation, 51
Work in Regress, 13-48
Workshop, 56

You know that it's time to pack up, 214
You say you *love* words, 56
You, whom I choose to dismiss in a distich, 296
Your *Weird* is beyond you, 171

Reading Peter Reading
ISABEL MARTIN

Reading Peter Reading is the first comprehensive study in English of Peter Reading's *œuvre*, illuminating its thematic and formal concerns, paradoxes and development as well as underlining its major status in contemporary literature. The book is based on Isabel Martin's pioneering doctoral dissertation on Reading, awarded the State Prize of Kiel University. Its updated, detailed textual analysis will help readers' understanding of the poetry, and as a whole it provides a thorough and substantial basis for any future critical discussion of Reading's works. Published in 2000, it covers all Reading's books from *Water and Waste* to *Marfan*.

ISABEL MARTIN read English and Russian at Kiel, Cambridge and Moscow Universities. She is a literary critic who lectures part-time at Koblenz University, as well as working as a freelance teacher trainer, translator and interpreter.

'A comprehensive survey of the poet's work over the last quarter of a century…Martin proves a lively reader, and does much to illuminate Reading's use of form and metre. Martin draws on a wide range of unpublished material including interviews and conversations with the poet. Her extensive knowledge of Reading's work allows for an interesting analysis of the "fastidious intratextuality" of the more recent volumes' – NEIL CHILTON, *Thumbscrew*.

'She does much to remind us what a superb prosodist he is. More than any poet writing today. Reading has revitalised classical metres for English use, which makes the comment of a Whitbread Prize judge in 1986 that "It doesn't even scan" all the more comically oafish…It is with Martin's book that all future studies of Reading will start' – DAVID WHEATLEY, *Times Literary Supplement*.

'The essential source book for any future discussion of Reading's work' – LAURIE SMITH, *Magma*.

'This is a major contribution – probably the most important so far – to the burgeoning field of Peter Reading Studies' – PHIL SIMMONS, *Poetry Quarterly Review*.

For a complete catalogue of Bloodaxe titles, please write to:
Bloodaxe Books Ltd, Highgreen, Tarset, Northumberland NE48 1RP